WAYS To GROW

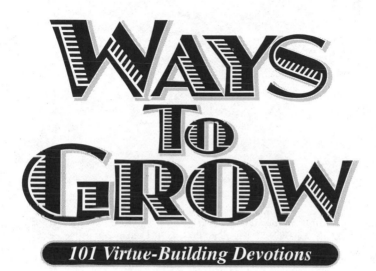

WAYS TO GROW

101 Virtue-Building Devotions

Eldon Weisheit

CPH
SAINT LOUIS

Scripture quotations are from the Good News Bible, the Bible in TODAY'S ENGLISH VER-
SION. Copyright © American Bible Society 1966, 1971, 1976. Used by permission.

Copyright © 1997 Concordia Publishing House
3558 S. Jefferson Avenue, St. Louis, MO 63118-3968
Manufactured in the United States of America

Library of Congress Cataloging-in-Publication Data

Weisheit, Eldon.
    Ways to grow : 101 virtue-building devotions / Eldon Weisheit.
        p.   cm.
    Summary: A collection of devotions based on real-life situations, focusing on relation-
ships, moral issues, and life's struggles in the light of Jesus and his resurrection.
    ISBN 0-570-04887-7
    1. Family—Prayer books and devotions—English. 2. Virtues—Meditations. 3. Christian
education—Home training. 4. Children—Religious life. 5. Children—Conduct of life.
6. Christian education of children. [1. Prayer books and devotions. 2. Christian life.
3. Conduct of life.] I. Title.
BV4526.2.W45   1997
249—dc20   96-41015

1   2   3   4   5   6   7   8   9   10   06   05   04   03   02   01   00   99   98   97

Contents

Preface

For the most important people, the children and the families who read this book, the goals for writing it are discussed by the fictional family in the first three devotions. There readers will learn *about* the stories in this book and how to make better use of them.

But for those parents, teachers, and others who want to know up front how to use this book with children, let me say that all the stories in it have two main purposes. One is to provide a tool to help individual children and families think about a variety of subjects and then talk about these things with each other and with others. The second purpose of every story is to help children recognize that Jesus, their Savior and Friend, is a part of their lives. Jesus will not be mentioned in each story, but He is there. By using the Bible reading, discussion questions, and the prayer, children will learn to recognize that Jesus is with them in everyday events.

Some of the stories also have special purposes: Most parents and teachers recognize that children must deal with drugs, alcohol, sex, and violence as well as other problems much earlier than their generation did. Children need guidance in making wise decisions even before they are confronted with these issues. And so some of these devotions address these topics. Many of the stories that do not overtly mention such topics are also designed to help children deal with the problems of society. The best education for young children about such topics as sex and drugs is that which teaches a faith in Jesus Christ;

which teaches them about repentance, forgiveness, and acceptance; and which helps children develop self-esteem and personal values rooted in God's love.

As children become teenagers, and as teenagers become adults, it becomes obvious that many children were never taught to make good decisions. Many are not prepared to take the necessary steps toward maturity because the long flight of steps toward adulthood did not start early enough in childhood. Therefore many of these stories are about decision making. Parents: Give special attention to these stories. Discuss the decision-making methods you use in your own family and allow the children to participate.

Some of the stories in this book are just for fun. They are about happy things and about family members. Children should not see family devotion time only as one more experience of adults laying a lesson on them. They also need to experience fun things. They need to have a chance to hear the stories told by other family members, and they also need to have others listen to their stories.

A final word to adults who are involved in the lives of children. These stories are offered only as a starter set. Tell your own stories. Listen to the kids tell theirs.

In Christ,

Eldon Weisheit
Tucson, Arizona

Devotion 1

How wonderful it is, how pleasant, for
God's people to live together in harmony!
Psalm 133:1

There Are Other Families Like Ours

"Do we have dessert tonight?" Shana asked as she
cleaned her plate and noticed that the others in the family
were also about finished with dinner.

"Yes," said her mother. "We are celebrating tonight, so
we are having chocolate pie."

"Great," said Alan. "We haven't had chocolate pie for
so long I can't remember what it tastes like."

"In case you don't like it," said Debi, "I'll eat yours."

"Fat chance," answered Alan.

"What are we celebrating?" asked Debi, who wasn't
counting on any extra pie anyway.

"We have a new storybook," said their father. "We're
going to read a story each evening after dinner."

"Do we have to?" asked Shana.

"Since you put it that way," her mother said, "yes, you
have to. But I think you'll like these stories."

"Why?" asked Shana.

"Because many of the stories are about families like
ours," said her mother.

"Why would we want to read stories about people like
us?" asked Alan. "We know enough about each other
already—maybe too much."

"We want you to know there are other families that do

the things we do," said their father. "Families that believe in Jesus, go to church, eat dinner together, and pray together."

"We also want you to know that there are other families like ours," added their mother, "families that argue with one another, brothers and sisters who fight, parents who disagree with one another and who make mistakes, who worry about money, and who have other problems."

"You mean other families have dumb sisters too?" asked Alan.

"And mean brothers who say bad things?" asked Shana.

"Yes," said their mother, "but some families don't have both brothers and sisters. Some don't have two parents. But they are families because the people in these families love each other, help each other, and are willing to stay after dinner to read a book about themselves."

"Okay," Shana said. "Where's the book?"

"Here it is," said their father. "You get to start, Debi. Look through the list of story titles and pick one that you think might be about our family."

Some Questions

1. What is the best time for your family to be together?

2. What can you do on days when all of your family can't be together at the same time? (*Suggestion:* Each of you read the same story and talk about it later.)

Prayer: Dear Jesus, bless everyone who lives in our house and help us remember that You live here too. Amen.

Devotion 2

Children, it is your Christian duty to obey your parents always, for that is what pleases God. Parents, do not irritate your children, or they will become discouraged. Colossians 3:20–21

There Are Other Kinds of Families

"It's my turn to pick a story tonight," said Alan as the family finished dinner.

"Okay," said his mother. "Here's the book."

"I already looked at it," said Alan. "Lots of the stories are not about families like ours."

"That's another reason we want to read the book together," said their father. "We want you to know about people who don't live as we do and who do other kinds of things."

"Not every family has both a mother and a father," said their mother. "Some have only one child, and some have more children than we do, but they are still families."

"One of my friends at school thinks our family is strange because we don't have any stepparents," said Debi.

"Karla has two families," said Shana. "She lives with her mother and that family for one week, and then with her father and his family the next week."

"When I was your age, our family included my grandmother who lived with us," said their mother.

"When I grew up," said their father, "I had two stepsisters who lived with us during the summer and sometimes at Christmas."

"Does this book tell about all those different kinds of families?" asked Debi.

"I'm not sure," said their mother, "because there are so many kinds of families. But people who live together make a family. Sometimes they are not really related to one another, but they still love each other. That's what makes them a family."

"We want you to know about all kinds of families," said their father, "so you can enjoy your friends and their families. You can bring your friends to our home so they can learn about us, and you can go to their homes so you can learn about them."

"Okay," said Alan. "I've got the story picked out for tonight."

Some Questions

1. What can you do to help everyone in your home be a happy family?

2. Does your family have to be like others, or do others have to be like your family?

   Prayer: Dear God, we ask You to bless our family. Also please bless _____ *(each person may name other families).* In Jesus' name. Amen.

 ## Devotion 3

Sensible people will see trouble coming and avoid it, but an unthinking person will walk right into it and regret it later. Proverbs 22:3

I Want to Read the One about …

"It's Shana's turn to pick a story tonight," Father said. "Are you ready?"

"Sort of. I read some of the stories by myself last night. Then I found something. Did you know about this?" she asked as she showed the table of contents in the front of the book.

"Of course," said Alan. "We learned how to use a table of contents in school."

"It lists everything in the book," said Shana. "It tells the titles of the stories. Some are about Sunday school, and birthdays, and anger, and people who call each other bad names."

"I looked through the contents too," said their mother. "I've already picked out some subjects that I want to read about when it's my turn."

"Do adults get turns too?" asked Alan.

"We certainly do," said their mother. "I found a lot of things in the contents that I think our family should talk about."

"But then you have to talk about the ones we pick too," said Debi.

"Sounds fair to me," said their father.

"Let's mark the ones we have already read," said Shana. "That way we'll know which ones we've already used."

"And let's make a rule that Mother only gets to pick a story on the days that we have dessert," said Alan.

"I hope there's a story in here about boys who eat too much cake," said Debi.

Some Questions

1. What subjects do you think your family should discuss?

2. If you want to talk about something that is not in this book, could you make up a story about that idea?

Prayer: Holy Spirit, help us learn from the Bible readings, from these stories, and from each other. In Jesus' name. Amen.

 ## Devotion 4

A description of heaven: *Never again will they hunger or thirst; neither sun nor any scorching heat will burn them, because the Lamb [Jesus], who is in the center of the throne, will be their shepherd, and He will guide them to springs of life-giving water. And God will wipe away every tear from their eyes. Revelation 7:16–17*

Are There Swimming Pools in Heaven?

"Are there swimming pools in heaven?" Savannah asked her father as he was tucking her in bed one night.

"I never thought about it," her father said. "Why do you want to know?"

"Because I think it would be nice to have a swimming pool," Savannah said. Her father remembered that she had spent the afternoon with her friend Jeanie, whose family had a swimming pool.

"Did you enjoy swimming at Jeanie's house today?" he asked.

"Yes, it was fun," she said. "That's why I think it would be nice to have a pool in heaven. Don't you think so?"

"I know heaven will be a happy place," said her father. "We will be with Jesus and with each other. I'll like that."

"But we'll have to do something," Savannah said, "and I like to swim."

"I think God will give us lots of exciting things to do," said her father.

"What do you want to do in heaven?" she asked.

"I look at it this way," he replied. "Jesus is the one who invites us to heaven and died in our place so that we may join Him there. I figure that He'll make it a good place for us to be. I'll be glad to do whatever is on His list."

"If you want, you can come to the pool with me," Savannah said.

"Okay," her father said, "and just in case it works out that way, I'll let you go golfing with me."

Some Questions

1. What makes you very happy now?

2. What do you think will make you happy in heaven?

Prayer: Lord Jesus, thank You for being with us here and thank You for making a place for us with You in heaven. Amen.

Devotion 5

[Jesus said,] "For He [God] makes His sun to shine on bad and good people alike, and gives rain to those who do good and to those who do evil." Matthew 5:45

Doesn't God Want Me to Have a Happy Birthday?

When Suzy woke up, she heard rain on her window. She hurried to look outside. The sky was gray, and the rain fell slowly and continually as if it were in no hurry to stop. Suzy started to cry.

"What's the matter, sweetie?" asked her mother. "I came in to say happy birthday to you. I thought you would be happy."

"But it's raining," Suzy said as tears ran down her cheeks.

"Yes," said her mother. "I liked the sound of rain on the roof and windows when I woke up this morning."

"But it's my birthday," Suzy said. "We're going to have a party. I wanted to have balloons and things out in the yard. We were going to play games in the grass. Now we can't because it's all wet."

"Don't worry," said her mother. "We will still have the party and do all the things that we planned. We'll just have the party inside."

"But it won't be as much fun," said Suzy. "Doesn't God want me to have a happy birthday?"

"Of course God wants you to have a happy birthday," said her mother. "Why would you ask that?"

"Because it's raining on my special day," said Suzy. "If God wanted me to have a happy birthday, He would have made it a beautiful day with sunshine."

"But rain is a blessing from God too," said her mother.

"Don't tell me about the farmers and people who have gardens," said Suzy. "They could have rain on another day."

"But that would be someone else's birthday," said her mother. "Every day is someone's birthday."

"But my day is special 'cause we're having a party," said Suzy.

"Every day is special to God, and every person is special to Him too," said her mother. "We know God loves us because He sent Jesus to be our Savior, not because of the weather."

Suzy looked at her mother. The tears were gone. "Can we still put up balloons?" she asked.

"Of course," said her mother. "We'll even put some on the outside of the windows so you can watch the rain splash on them."

Some Questions

1. How do you know God loves you on sad days as well as on happy days? Can you find a Bible verse that tells you about God's love?

2. How do you know that we do not measure God's love by how rich or how healthy we are?

Prayer: Dear God, thank You for the day that You have given me. Please help me make it a good day for others too. In Jesus' name. Amen.

Devotion 6

[Jesus said,] "Ask, and you will receive;
seek, and you will find; knock, and the door
will be opened to you. For everyone who asks
will receive, and anyone who seeks will find,
and the door will be opened to him who
knocks." Matthew 7:7–8

Could Someone Pray?

Four families, including 11 children, went on a fishing trip at a state park. Everyone was having fun when they heard a scream. They all ran towards the sound and saw Ricky, a 4-year-old boy. He had tried to ride a bicycle. It had fallen over, and one of his fingers was caught in the spokes of a wheel.

"Don't bump the bike," someone screamed. "If the wheel turns, it will cut off his finger."

"Don't scare him," someone else said. "If he jerks his hand, he will lose the finger."

"Call 911!"

"The nearest phone is 10 miles away."

"The best thing to do is hold the bike steady so it won't tip," someone suggested.

"Hold real still, Ricky," his mother said.

"If someone has a rod, we could block the wheel so it won't turn," said Ricky's father.

"I've got some tools in my trunk," said someone else. "I'll see what I can find."

"Could we pray?" asked one of the children.

The adults stopped suddenly. They all realized that they had panicked. Everyone—even the children—was still for a moment.

"Yes, Sarah, we can pray," said Ricky's mother. "You pray for all of us."

Adults and children reached out to hold hands. Ricky's father reached to his son's free hand.

"Dear Jesus," prayed Sarah, "please help Ricky get his hand free. Amen."

Ricky's father reached over and slowly moved the wheel back. Ricky pulled his finger free and climbed into his father's arms.

"Thank you, Sarah," said one of the adults.

"I'm glad we don't have to drive 10 miles to reach God's 911," said another.

Some Questions

1. Do you remember to pray when you need help?

2. Do you have a special prayer that you say?

Prayer: Lord, teach us to pray. *(Add your prayers for your family and others.)* Amen.

Devotion 7

No more lying, then! Everyone must tell the truth to his fellow believer, because we are all members together in the body of Christ. Ephesians 4:25

My Teacher Told a Lie

"What did you do in school today?" Erin's mother asked as they walked toward home.

"My teacher told a lie," Erin answered.

"Are you sure?" her mother asked.

"Yes!"

"Sometimes we misunderstand something that someone said and think it is a lie," her mother said.

"No, Mrs. Lasher lied," said Erin. "When I got to my classroom, she was not there, but lots of kids were there. We waited for a long time. Then some of the boys started making noise. The principal came in and made us all sit at our desks. Then Mrs. Lasher came in. She told the principal that she had been there and had left to go to the bathroom. But she lied 'cause her purse and briefcase were not on her desk. After the principal left, she went out in the hall and got them."

Erin's mother didn't say anything as the two walked together.

"Do you think she lied, Mom?" Erin asked.

"It sounds as though she did," her mother answered. "Sometimes teachers, and even mothers and fathers, make mistakes."

"But you and Daddy tell me not to lie," Erin said. "Why can Mrs. Lasher lie?"

"It is wrong for her to lie," said her mother. "People who tell lies hurt themselves even more than they hurt the people they lie to. Mrs. Lasher is a good teacher and teaches you many good things. But she was wrong when she told a lie. You must learn the good things from her, not the bad."

"If I told a lie, you would make me stay in my room," Erin said. "Should Mrs. Lasher have to stay in her room?"

"The school principal will have to help Mrs. Lasher," said her mother. "I'm glad that you know lying is wrong. I also want you to know that Jesus helps you. When you do tell a lie, He forgives you. And He helps you want to tell the truth."

"What's for dinner tonight?" Erin asked.

"I cannot tell a lie," her mother answered. "I don't have the slightest idea what we are having for dinner."

Some Questions

1. If someone tells you a lie, does that mean it's okay for you to lie to that person?

2. Why do you get in trouble if you tell lies?

Prayer: Dear Jesus, thank You for forgiving me when I do bad things. Help me tell the truth all the time. Amen.

 ## Devotion 8

Your word is a lamp to guide me and a light for my path. I will keep my solemn promise to obey Your just instructions.
Psalm 119:105–106

Why Do You Go to Sunday School?

Rick and Jimmy were putting the Nintendo game away. Rick had won today, but when they played last Saturday, Jimmy had won.

"Come over again next Saturday," Jimmy said, "and I'll beat you good."

"Why wait a whole week?" Rick answered. "I'll come over tomorrow morning—unless you're afraid that I'll win again."

"Can't tomorrow," Jimmy said. "I'm going to Sunday school."

"Why do you go to Sunday school?" Rick asked. "Don't you get enough of school during the week?"

"Sunday school is different," Jimmy explained.

"How is it different?"

"There are different kids and a different teacher," answered Jimmy. "And we talk about different kinds of things."

"What kinds of things?" Rick asked.

"About God and stuff like that."

"Why do you want to talk about those kinds of things?" Rick asked.

"I like to know about God," Jimmy said. "He sent Jesus to be our Savior—that's what we talked about last week."

"My dad said that only sissies go to church," Rick said.

"Would you call Mr. Brandon a sissy?" Jimmy asked. Mr. Brandon was the football coach for the big kids at Rick and Jimmy's school.

"No," said Rick. "Not even when he couldn't hear me."

"He goes to my church," said Jimmy. "He's my sister's

Sunday school teacher. You want to go with us tomorrow?"

"I'll ask my mom."

Some Questions

1. What do you know about Sunday school?

2. Do you know anyone who might like to go to Sunday school with you?

Prayer: Dear Jesus, bless all the people who teach Sunday school and all the children who attend. Amen.

 ## Devotion 9

We want you to know the truth about those who have died, so that you will not be sad, as are those who have no hope. We believe that Jesus died and rose again, and so we believe that God will take back with Jesus those who have died believing in Him.
1 Thessalonians 4:13–14

Did I Wear a Pigeon Suit?

"Look, Grandpa!" said Julian. "Here's my pigeon suit." Julian held up a child-size rented tuxedo. "I get to wear it for Uncle Dirk's wedding!"

"Dirk told him they were wearing penguin suits," Julian's mother explained to answer the puzzled look on her father-in-law's face. "He got his birds mixed up."

While the other family members talked about details of the upcoming wedding, Julian and his grandfather walked out in the backyard.

"Are you going to wear a pigeon suit to the wedding, Grandpa?" Julian asked.

"No," Grandfather answered. "I'll get by with my regular black suit this time. But I wore one to my wedding."

"What did I wear at your wedding?" Julian asked.

"You weren't at my wedding," Grandfather answered.

"Where was I?" the boy asked.

"You weren't born yet."

"Couldn't I have been born then so I could go to your wedding?" Julian asked.

"No, grandpas are always born a long time before their grandchildren."

"Why?"

"Because that's how we get to help each other. I was born a long time before you so I could be old now and know a lot of things to tell you while you are little," Grandfather answered. "With the stories that my father and grandfather told me, I can tell you about things that happened 100 years ago!"

"I can tell you stories too."

"Sure you can," the old man answered. "You can tell me about the things you want to do when you grow up, about when you have a little child or a grandchild."

"Will you tell them stories too?" Julian asked.

"No, I'll be dead by then."

"I don't want you to die."

"I probably won't die for a long time," Grandfather said. "But it's okay when I do because I'll be ready to live in heaven with Jesus."

"Can I come to heaven to be with you and Jesus too?" Julian asked.

"Someday," Grandfather answered. "But just as I got to live a long time before you were born, you get to live a long time after I die."

"Can we wear pigeon suits in heaven?" Julian asked.

"I never thought about that," the old man said. "But I tell you what—when I get there, I'll ask. If they have any, I'll keep one for you."

Some Questions

1. Do the children have any questions about death that they want to ask?

2. What stories about a dead relative should your children know?

Prayer: Lord Jesus, thank You for giving Your life on the cross so we may all be with You in heaven. Amen.

 Devotion 10

I think of days gone by and remember years of long ago. Psalm 77:5

A Day to Remember

"Today is a special day for me," Kevin and Leah's mother said as she gave them orange juice for breakfast.

"Every Saturday is a special day," said Kevin, "because

we don't have to go to school."

"But this is a special Saturday," their mother said. "I remember what I did 28 years ago today."

"Is it someone's birthday?" Leah asked.

"No," said Mother. "But birthdays are nice too."

"What did you do 28 years ago today?" Leah asked.

"It was a Saturday then too," she answered. "My mother was fixing soup for lunch, and I said I didn't want soup. So she asked me what I would like to have for lunch. I told her I wanted hot dogs, french fries, and chocolate chip cookies. She put the soup in the refrigerator. Then we went to the store. We bought foot-long hot dogs, potatoes, and all the things to make cookies. We peeled the potatoes and made french fries. We baked enough cookies to last a week."

"That sounds good," said Kevin. "But do you remember that day because you had something fun to eat?"

"No, I remember it because my mother spent the whole day with me. She did the things I wanted to do even though she had other things to do. That made me happy. I want you two to have a happy day today."

"Are we going to have hot dogs and french fries for lunch?" Leah asked.

"If you want," Mother said. "But that was *my* special day. You may want to do something else. I want to do what you want to do so you can remember this day many years from now."

Leah and Kevin looked at each other and smiled. Their mother could tell that they were thinking the same thing. "What do you want to do?" she asked.

"Will you climb the tree with us?" Kevin asked.

"Which tree?" asked their mother.

"That one out there," said Leah as she pointed out the kitchen window.

For a moment their mother looked a little scared. Then she thought about the day 28 years before when she was 9 years old. "Okay," she said. "Let's go climb the tree."

The three of them ran out into the backyard. Leah and Kevin led the way up the lower branches of the big tree. At first their mother struggled to keep up, but once she got to the third limb she remembered the joy of tree climbing. The three of them went higher and higher. They laughed as they saw the dog in a yard two blocks away. Each of their minds was filled with a memory that would make this day special for the rest of their lives.

Some Questions

1. What are some special things that every member of your family remembers?

2. What would you like to do to build future memories?

   Prayer: Lord Jesus, help us remember this day because You are with us and we are with You. Amen.

 ## Devotion 11

Put into practice what you learned and received from me, both from my words and from my actions. And the God who gives us peace will be with you. Philippians 4:9

You Decided What to Do

Tony and his mother sat at the kitchen table. They had planned a good Saturday. Both of them remembered how they had looked forward to this day. Tony's mother had an office luncheon to attend. It was a big event for her, and she was going to get a baby-sitter. But Tony said he was big enough to stay by himself, and he asked if his best friend, Adam, could stay with him. His mother knew Adam and felt that the boys could be trusted together. The two boys agreed that they would not leave the house while Tony's mother was gone.

Tony's mother was happy when she came home from the party—until she walked into the house. There she saw three boys with a neighbor—Mr. Dobbs. Mr. Dobbs explained that he had found the three boys smoking cigarettes in his garage.

Tony explained what had happened. Adam had phoned his friend Josh and asked him to come over. Josh brought cigarettes. The other boys were going to smoke them, and Tony knew his mother would smell smoke in the house—so they went to Mr. Dobbs' garage.

"I'm sorry," Tony said after everyone had gone home.

"I know you are sorry," said his mother, "and I forgive you. But we have a problem because you didn't do what I told you to do."

"It's not my fault," said Tony. "Adam invited Josh to come over. And Josh had the cigarettes."

"They were wrong too," his mother said. "But you made two bad decisions. You should not have agreed with Adam to invite Josh. I trusted you without a baby-sitter. I gave you a responsibility, and you didn't live up to it. You also should have told Josh he couldn't bring cigarettes into our house. You know I would not have allowed it. Adam's mother wouldn't have either."

"I'll do better next time," said Tony.

"I want you to learn how to make decisions for yourself, Tony," his mother said. "Now I can make you obey, but as you grow older, you have to decide things for yourself. I made a mistake this week when I decided to let you stay home without a sitter. You made a mistake when you let Adam invite Josh to our house. We both have to learn."

"I will never do it again," Tony said.

"You are going to be grounded for all of next week," his mother said. "We both will think about it, and we'll talk again next Saturday about making decisions."

Some Questions

1. What have the people in your family done to help you trust each other?

2. What do you do when someone breaks the trust you have in your family?

Prayer: Lord Jesus, when we do wrong, forgive us. Help us to forgive and trust one another. Amen.

Devotion 12

We belong to God. Whoever knows God listens to us; whoever does not belong to God does not listen to us. This, then, is how we can tell the difference between the Spirit of truth and the spirit of error. 1 John 4:6

How Will I Know?

Tony was grounded for a week because he broke the promise he had made to his mother when she let him stay at home without a sitter. At home Tony was quiet, and he tried to do the right things to help his mother. At school Tony looked happy, but he felt sad inside. Adam's family invited Tony to play miniature golf with them on Saturday. But Tony didn't even ask his mother if he could go. He knew that he was grounded.

On Saturday afternoon Tony and his mother sat down at the kitchen table again.

"Tony, you are a good boy," his mother said. "I love you very much."

"I love you too, Mom," Tony said.

"I know," she answered. "Because I love you, I want to protect you from trouble. I don't want anyone to hurt you, and even more, I don't want you to hurt yourself."

"I'd never hurt myself," Tony said.

"You hurt yourself last week," his mother said. "You hurt yourself even more than you hurt me when you broke your promise. You hurt yourself when you smoked cigarettes. They are bad for you. My Uncle Ray died when he was only 50 years old because he started smoking when he was a child."

"Mom, I only took a couple of puffs," said Tony, "and it made me sick."

"Oh, I know," said his mother. "I understand that you have to try some things. And I know you can't be perfect—I'm not either. But I want you to learn how to make decisions for yourself. You will need to know how to pick friends. You have to learn to decide things for yourself rather than following others."

"You can help me, Mom," Tony said.

"Yes, I can help you," she answered, "but I have to help you by teaching you how to make your own decisions. You will want to drive a car. You need to know how to drive safely. You will have to make decisions about alcohol and drugs and sex. You need to know how to enjoy life by doing those things that are good for everyone all the time, rather than those things that seem good just for the moment."

"How will I know?"

"That's why I teach you about Jesus," his mother said. "Jesus helps you two ways. He died on the cross to take the punishment for the wrong decisions that you make. He forgives you when you're wrong. And Jesus helps you decide how to do the right things. He's your Friend. When you're with good friends, you'll do good things. He's the best Friend."

Some Questions

1. Do you know some bad decisions that you have made?
2. Have you learned anything good from decisions you have made?

Prayer: Dear God, thank You for sending Jesus to be with me. Help me talk with Him and walk with Him. Amen.

 Devotion 13

Remember, O LORD, Your kindness and constant love which You have shown from long ago. Psalm 25:6

I ... AM ... A ... ROBOT

"Grandpa, remember how I used to ride on your shoulders when we went for a walk?" Julian asked as they walked home from a ball game.

"Yes," his grandpa answered, "but that was when you were a little boy. We've both outgrown that now."

"Tell me a story about when I was a little boy," Julian said.

"Okay," Grandpa said. "Once upon a time, when you were about 3, you came over to our house. When you came in, I said, 'Hi, Julian.'

" 'I ... AM ... NOT ... JULIAN,' you said. 'I ... AM ... A ... ROBOT.'

" 'What's your name, robot?' I asked.

" 'ROBOTS ... DO ... NOT ... HAVE ... NAMES,' you said.

" 'What do I call you?' I asked.

" 'YOU ... CALL ... ME ... ROBOT,' you answered. Then you pushed an imaginary button on your chest and said, 'PSSSSSSKKKKEEEWWY.'

" 'Did you blow up, robot?' I asked.

" 'NO,' you answered, 'YOU ... DID.' "

The old man and the young boy laughed.

"Did I really say that?" Julian asked.

"YES ... YOU ... DID," answered his grandpa.

Some Questions

1. What can you remember about yourself when you were very little?

2. Who can tell you stories about you that you do not remember by yourself?

Prayer: Holy Spirit, thank You for making me God's child. Be with me all of my life. In Jesus' name. Amen.

Devotion 14

A good man's words are a fountain of life, but a wicked man's words hide a violent nature.
Proverbs 10:11

I'm the Shortest Kid in My Class

Jon liked to talk to Mr. Mueller who lived next door. Mr. Mueller was retired, so he had time to spend with kids.

"Did you know I'm the shortest kid in my class?" Jon asked Mr. Mueller one day.

"No," Mr. Mueller said, "I didn't know that. Did your

teacher have a contest or something?"

"What do you mean?" Jon asked.

"I wondered how you found out you were the shortest kid in your class," the old man said. "Did you all stand up in a row with the tallest person on one end and the shortest on the other?"

"No, I figured it out by myself," said Jon. "Blair is the tallest. Lots of girls are even taller than I am."

"So I guess you win the prize," said Mr. Mueller.

"What prize?" asked Jon.

"The first-place prize for being the shortest."

"No, you don't understand," said Jon. "They give the prize to the *tallest* person."

"Who said so?" Mr. Mueller asked.

"Everybody knows that," said Jon.

"I didn't know that," said the old man, "and I am someone."

"Well, I'd rather be the tallest one," Jon said.

"Would that make you a better person?"

"I think so," said Jon.

"I don't think so," said Mr. Mueller. "You are who you are. I know your family. Do you like your Uncle Roger?"

"He's neat," said Jon.

"Is he tall?"

"No, he's short," said Jon.

"Do you want to change him and make him tall?" asked Mr. Mueller.

"No, I like him the way he is," said Jon.

"And I like you the way you are," said Mr. Mueller. "What I mean is—God knew what He was doing when He made us. We don't need to mess around with worrying how well He did His job."

"You're smart," said Jon.

"Maybe so, maybe not," said Mr. Mueller. "Would you like me if I weren't so smart?"

Some Questions

1. Why do some people worry about being short or tall?

2. Can you name some good things about yourself?

Prayer: Dear God, thank You for making me just as I am. Help me be a good kid now and help me become a good teenager someday. In Jesus' name. Amen.

 ## Devotion 15

You are so rich in all you have: in faith, speech, and knowledge, in your eagerness to help and in your love for us. And so we want you to be generous also in this service of love. 2 Corinthians 8:7

Do I Have to Give Her a Gift?

Marshall was surprised to find a letter addressed to him when he came home from school. It was an invitation to Kristin's birthday party. He was happy about the party. It was on a Saturday afternoon, so he wouldn't have to spend the whole day helping his parents do chores. He was sure that his friends from school would be at the party too.

"Can I go to the birthday party?" Marshall asked his mother.

"Sure you can," she said. "Do you want to buy a gift for Kristin by yourself, or do you want me to help?"

"Do I have to give her a gift?" he asked.

"No, you never *have* to give a gift," said his mother. "If you *had* to give a gift, it wouldn't be a gift."

"Then I don't want to give her anything," the boy said.

"Why do you think Kristin invited you to her party?" his mother asked.

"Because I'm her friend, I guess," he answered.

"Sometimes people like to invite their friends to parties," said his mother, "and sometimes people like to give their friends birthday gifts."

"You mean it is the polite thing to do," Marshall said because he knew his mother was into politeness.

"Yes, it is," said his mother, "but it's more than that. Taking a gift to a party helps you learn how to give. That's an important lesson in life."

"But I know how to give, Mom," said Marshall. "You just say, 'Here, I've got something for you.' "

"That's part of it," said his mother. "But you also need to learn how to pick a gift for that special person, and you want that person to know that you thought of her. I think it is fun to see someone enjoy a gift that I gave."

"Kristin likes the same kind of music that I do," said Marshall. "I could get her a CD. I know she has a player in her room."

"Would you like to get her a CD?" his mother asked.

"I'd better check to see if I have enough money," Marshall said.

"Good idea," said his mother.

Some Questions

1. What gifts have you received that you especially enjoy?

2. What gifts have you enjoyed giving to others?

Prayer: Holy Spirit, give me the gift of giving so I may enjoy giving to others and can appreciate what others give to me. In Jesus' name. Amen.

 ## Devotion 16

Be joyful always, pray at all times, be thankful in all circumstances. This is what God wants from you in your life in union with Christ Jesus. 1 Thessalonians 5:16–18

He Says We Can't Pray in School

Sharon and Jake had an argument on the way home from school. They decided to ask their mother who was right.

"Mom," Sharon said as soon as she came into the house, "Jake says we can't pray at school, and I say we can. Who is right?"

"Well, what caused this argument?" asked their mother as she went to the refrigerator to get their snack.

"Remember last night when we had family devotions?" asked Jake. "Both of us said we were having big tests in school, and we asked God to help us. Then you said we still had to study for the tests but that we could pray again before the tests."

"Yes, I remember all of that," their mother answered.

"When we got close to school today, I said we should stop and pray before we went in," said Jake. "But Sharon said she was going to wait and pray while the teacher gave out the papers. I told her we couldn't pray in school."

"And I told him I could pray wherever I wanted to," said Sharon, "and I did too."

"But I heard it on the news," said Jake. "They said there is a law against praying in school. So I know I am right."

"But I remember what I learned in Sunday school," said Sharon. "My teacher said we could pray all the time. So I know *I'm* right."

"I'm glad to have a problem like this," said their mother. "By the way, I remembered what we talked about last night, and I prayed for you today too."

"But you aren't answering our question," said Jake.

"Jake, what you heard on TV meant that the entire class could not pray together," said their mother. "In our country, we protect our religious freedom. We want to pray to God in our own way. We don't want schools or laws telling us to pray or not to pray."

"See, I told you I was right," said Jake.

"Wait a minute," said their mother. "Sharon is also right. The class cannot pray together, but anyone who wants to pray alone may. You can pray before a test by talking to God from your heart. God hears your thoughts.

You can pray before you eat lunch or anytime."

"You mean we have to hide our prayer?" asked Sharon.

"No, you need never be ashamed to pray," said their mother, "but you don't need to show off that you pray either. Pray when you want to talk to God. You can do that anytime, anyplace, and He'll always listen."

Some Questions

1. Can you name different times and places where you have prayed?

2. How can God hear you if you don't talk out loud?

Prayer: Dear God, thanks for hearing our prayer now. Help us to be always tuned in to talk to You. In Jesus' name. Amen.

 ## Devotion 17

You created every part of me; You put me together in my mother's womb. I praise You because You are to be feared; all You do is strange and wonderful. I know it with all my heart. Psalm 139:13–14

Who Are You?

"Who are you?" the father said as he picked up his daughter and swung her in the air, then held her close.

"I am Libby!" she answered.

"Who is Libby?" he asked.

"I am your sweet little girl," she answered.

"Is that all?"

"I am Mommy's sweet little girl too," she said. "And I am Grandpa and Grandma's sweet little girl."

"And?"

"I am Scott's big sister, and I am Uncle Norm and Aunt Debbie's niece," she said.

By now the father was sitting down with his daughter in his lap. They had played the game many times before, and both knew it was not over.

"You must be a very special little girl," the father said, "because we all love you so much. Who else are you?"

"I am God's little girl. He made me," Libby said.

"That's a new one," said her father. "That's good. Where did you learn that?"

"Mommy told me," she said. "And that's what my Sunday school teacher says too."

"What else does your Sunday school teacher tell you?"

"She says Jesus loves me and He died on the cross for me," the little girl answered.

"Are you a happy little girl?"

"Yes!"

"Why?"

"Because I love everybody who loves me," she said. "Jesus too!"

Some Questions

1. Who are the most important people in your life?

2. Why is God important in your life?

Prayer: Thank You, God, for creating me and all the people around me. In Jesus' name. Amen.

Devotion 18

*I remember the sincere faith you have, the
kind of faith that your grandmother Lois and
your mother Eunice also had. I am sure that
you have it also. For this reason I remind you
to keep alive the gift that God gave you when
I laid my hands on you. 2 Timothy 1:5–6*

Is That Why You Believe in Jesus?

"How'd the ball game go today?" Julian's grandfather
asked.

"Not very well," Julian answered. "I struck out once,
got left on base twice, and I dropped a ball when Nick
threw it to me."

"Doesn't sound like a good game," said his grandfather.

"We lost, 12-2," said Julian. "Did you play ball when
you were a kid, Grandpa?"

"I tried," said his grandfather, "but I was a klutz. I
never played well."

"Didn't you ever have a good game?" Julian asked.

"Yes, once," said his grandfather as he sat down. Julian
sat beside him because he knew his grandfather had a
story to tell.

"I remember one day," said the grandfather. "Two big
boys chose up sides, just as they always did. I was the
last one chosen, just as I always was. They even took
some of the girls before me."

"No, they didn't," said Julian.

"Yes, they did," said his grandfather. "The big kids put me in the outfield so I wouldn't be in the way. I watched as the other team got runners on second and third bases. Then I prayed. I asked God to let the batter hit a fly ball to me. And to let me catch it. That would be one out and one miracle. And to let the runner on second base head for third because he wouldn't think I could catch the ball. That wouldn't be a miracle. And to let me tag second— that would be the second out and the second miracle. Then to let me throw the ball straight to the third base- man for the third miracle and the third out.

"I was just ready to say 'in Jesus' name,' " said Grandpa, "when I heard a loud crack. I forgot about praying and reached for the ball, caught it, and tagged second. Then I threw it to third, and there were three outs. When I walked off the field, I thought Jesus had His arm around my shoulders."

"Is that why you believe in Jesus and go to church?" asked Julian.

"No, I never thought of it that way," said Grandpa. "I believe in Jesus because He is my Savior. I know He loves me because He died for me, not because He helped me win a ball game."

"Can I pray that way too?" asked Julian.

"Sure, you can," said Grandpa. "But I should tell you that God hasn't answered all of my prayers the way He did that one. As I grew older, I started to think that my ball-game prayer was a little selfish. Then it dawned on me. Jesus was a little kid one time too. I bet He played on teams that lost. I think He understood how I felt, and I think He understands how you feel."

"That's a good story, Grandpa," said Julian.

"Yes, it is," his grandpa answered. "But now it's time to work on your catching. Get your glove. We've got work to do."

Some Questions

1. Does God love you even when your team loses or you have other problems?

2. What do you ask God to help you do?

Prayer: Lord Jesus, thank You for listening to my prayers. Thank You for giving me the answers that are best. Amen.

 ## Devotion 19

Everything I fear and dread comes true. I have no peace, no rest, and my troubles never end. Job 3:25–26

On a Bad Day

Richard was angry when he came home from school. Everything had gone wrong. He had forgotten to take his homework to school, and the teacher had scolded him. He spilled milk on himself at lunch. He felt so bad that he yelled at his best friend, and his friend had played with some other kids during recess.

When he walked into his house, his dog, Freddie, jumped on him and wanted to play.

"Get out of here," Richard said as he pushed Freddie

away. "You're always such a pest."

"What's wrong with you today?" his mother asked. Richard always liked to play with his dog.

"There's nothing wrong with me," Richard said. "Why are you picking on me too?"

"I didn't mean to pick on you," said his mother. "I could see that you weren't happy, and I wanted to help you."

"Then leave me alone," said Richard. "I don't like to be nagged."

"Wait just a minute, Son," said his mother. "I can tell you've had a bad day, but you can't talk to me or anyone else that way."

"Why not?" asked Richard. "Everyone else talks to me that way."

Just then Richard's sister, Karla, came into the kitchen.

"Get out of here," Richard yelled. "I was here first."

"I just came in to get a drink," protested Karla.

"You're going to bug me, I know," said Richard. "You always do."

"That's enough," said their mother. "Richard, go to your room. I'll be in later."

"Why don't you just lock me in there?" Richard said as he slammed the bedroom door.

His mother waited for about half an hour, then knocked on Richard's door.

"Go away," he said.

"No, you and I are going to have a talk," said his mother. She came into the room and turned off his radio.

"Leave that on," said Richard.

"No," said his mother. "You came home from school

with a big problem. I'm sorry that you had a bad day. But you made it worse by being unkind to your dog, to me, and to your sister. I don't know what caused your first problem, but you are adding to the problems you have."

"Miss Clevenger doesn't treat me fairly at school," said Richard. "And Scott wouldn't play with me at recess."

"I can understand that you feel bad about that," said his mother. "But that has nothing to do with your pet, your sister, or me."

"I didn't want to be with anyone when I came home," said Richard.

"Okay. Then you should have said, 'I'm in a bad mood,' and gone to your room."

Richard didn't say anything.

"I'm going to leave you alone for a while," said his mother. "I want you to think about whatever happened today. Then think of ways you could have made it a better day."

Some Questions

1. What do you do to help yourself when you have a bad day? How will Jesus help you?

2. What can you do to help others when they have a bad day?

Prayer: Jesus, please be with me when I'm scared, angry, jealous, and all those other things that make me feel alone. That's when I really need You. Amen.

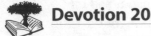

Devotion 20

By our baptism, then, we were buried with Him and shared His death, in order that, just as Christ was raised from death by the glorious power of the Father, so also we might live a new life. Romans 6:4

I'm in a Bad Mood

Richard remembered to take his homework to school the next day. Scott played with him at recess. When he came home from school, he was happy. He played with Freddie, then played his Nintendo game with Karla.

But the next Monday things went wrong again. He had talked his mother into letting him stay up late Sunday night to watch a movie, so he was tired. He didn't understand what Miss Clevenger was talking about in social studies. The cafeteria served cold macaroni and cheese for lunch. It tasted like rubber.

"It's my turn to be team captain," Scott told him as they went out for recess. Richard was going to argue. Then he remembered what his mother had said.

"I'm in a bad mood today," Richard said.

"Okay," said Scott. "You don't have to play."

It worked! That afternoon when he got home from school, his mother asked him to clean up all of the litter in the alley behind their house.

"I'm in a bad mood today," he said.

"Okay," said his mother. "You can rest a while. But you must do it before dinner."

Richard got lonely in his room, so he went to his sister's room.

"Get out of here!" Karla yelled. Her friend, Jenny, from across the street was with her.

"This is my house too," Richard said.

"But this is my room, and my friend is here," said Karla.

"I'm in a bad mood today," said Richard.

"Tough," said his sister. "Get out of here. Mom! Make Richard get out of here."

Their mother came down the hall.

"What's going on here?" she asked.

"Richard is pestering me and Jenny," said Karla.

"I was not," said Richard. "You told me to say, 'I'm in a bad mood,' and I did."

"I'm sorry you're in a bad mood," said his mother, "and I'm glad that you know it. But that doesn't mean you should make us all unhappy."

"I don't have anything to do," said Richard.

"Yes, you do," said his mother. "Clean the alley!"

Some Questions

1. If someone else is in a bad mood, do you get in a bad mood too?

2. What are some of the things you can do to make yourself and others feel better? How will Jesus help you?

Prayer: Jesus, help me be a happy person and give me a good attitude. Thank You for forgiving me when I'm in a bad mood. Amen.

Devotion 21

How can we sing a song to the LORD in a
foreign land? May I never be able to play
the harp again if I forget you, Jerusalem!
Psalm 137:4–5

You've Been Everywhere!

Jake and Ronnie were glad that school was out. They celebrated the first day of vacation by climbing as high as they could in the big tree in Jake's backyard.

"This is fun," said Jake. "I know what we should do this summer. Let's count how many trees we can climb in our neighborhood."

"That sounds like fun," said Ronnie, "but we'll have to do it fast because next week I'm going to visit my grandma in Chicago."

"You're always going somewhere," said Jake. "Don't you ever want to stay here?"

"Sure I do," said Ronnie. "I like living here. But I used to live by my grandma's house, and I have lots of relatives and friends in Chicago."

"When will you be back?" asked Jake.

"I think we're going to be there about 10 days," said Ronnie. "But in July I get to go to Texas to stay with Uncle Bernie. I go there every summer."

"You've been everywhere," said Jake. "I've never been anywhere but here."

"I've already gone to four schools, and I've lived in five states," said Ronnie.

"I wish I could move somewhere else," said Jake. "I'm tired of this town."

"But you've got all of your family here," said Ronnie. "I wish I could see my grandparents and cousins every week the way you do."

"You mean you wish you had always lived in one place?" asked Jake.

"Sure," his friend answered. "You don't wish that you had moved around to all of those places like I have, do you?"

"That sounds like fun to me," said Jake.

"That's funny," said Ronnie. "I want to do what you did, and you want to do what I did. I'm glad I know someone who has lived in one house all his life. I like that."

"And I know someone who has lived in lots of places," said Jake. "I like that."

Some Questions

1. How many places have you lived?

2. Would you rather move to lots of different places or always stay in one home?

3. Do you know other families that have moved more times (and fewer times) than your family?

Prayer: Thank You, God, for the home and friends I have now and for homes and friends I used to have. Bless the homes and friends I will have in the future. In Jesus' name. Amen.

Devotion 22

Because of His love God had already decided that through Jesus Christ He would make us His sons—this was His pleasure and purpose. Let us praise God for His glorious grace, for the free gift He gave us in His dear Son! Ephesians 1:4b–6

Who Would Be You?

Jenny's mother picked her up at Ericka's house. Jenny had spent the night with her friend.

"Did you have fun with Ericka?" Mom asked as they drove toward home.

"We had lots of fun," said Jenny. "Last night we talked about who we'd like to be."

"And who would you like to be?" asked her mother.

"At first I wanted to be Miss Desmond, my teacher," said Jenny.

"Then?" her mother asked.

"After Ericka said she wanted to be the woman who won the gold medal for skating, I changed my mind. I want to be a tennis player and win a gold medal. But do you want to know the dumb thing that happened?"

"What happened?" asked her mother.

"While Ericka and I were talking about who we would like to be, her little brother came into her room. He said—you won't believe this—he said he wanted to be Jimmy—my brother, Jimmy! Can you believe that?"

"Yes," said her mom. "Jimmy's a teenager. He's a good

athlete, and he gets good grades at school. I can see that a little boy would want to be like him."

"But Jimmy is a pest," said Jenny. "He yells at me. He's messy, and he wears stupid clothes."

"But think about the people you would like to be," said her mother. "You've only seen Miss Desmond in the classroom. You've only seen the others on TV. Maybe if you lived with them, you wouldn't want to be like them either."

"But they couldn't be as bad as Jimmy," said Jenny.

Her mom laughed. "It's fun to play pretend, but I want you to be you."

"What do you mean?" asked Jenny.

"If you were Miss Desmond, or if you were a famous tennis player, then I wouldn't have you. I want you to be who you are because you are very special to me—and to lots of other people too."

Jenny sat quietly for awhile.

"I like being me too," she said.

Some Questions

1. Do you sometimes like to pretend you are someone else?

2. What kind of people do you pick as the ones you want to be like?

3. Why might other people want to be like you?

Prayer: Thank You, God, for making me who I am. Help me to enjoy other people and to follow good examples. In Jesus' name. Amen.

Devotion 23

Meanwhile these three remain: faith, hope, and love; and the greatest of these is love.
1 Corinthians 13:13

It's an Empty Box

Jeff and Mindy were excited because their grandmother came to their house for her birthday. For a whole week each of them had planned a special birthday gift for their grandmother. They kept their gifts a secret—even from each other. Their mother had taken them to the store so they could use part of their allowance to buy the presents.

Finally, the time came for Grandmother to open the gifts. Jeff had wrapped his gift in some bright paper. Grandmother unwrapped that gift slowly.

"Thank you, Jeff," she said as she saw the bracelet he had bought for her. She gave him a big hug. "This will be beautiful with the new dress I gave myself for my birthday."

Then Mindy handed her grandmother a bright red box. Jeff had seen the box in Mindy's sack and wondered what was in it. She was younger and received a smaller allowance. Jeff couldn't guess what was in it.

Grandma took her time as she lifted the lid off the box.

"There's nothing in it," Jeff said. "It's an empty box. That's not a present."

"Yes, it is," said Mindy. "The box is the present. I thought it was pretty. I knew Grandma would like it."

"It is beautiful, Mindy," said Grandma. " I do like it."

"But it's an empty box," said Jeff.

"No, it is not empty," said Grandma. "It is filled with love and thoughtfulness. I like the box. See how I can use it. The bracelet you gave me fits in it just right. I will keep the bracelet in this box on my dresser. That way when I use either gift, I will think of both of you. You have made me very happy on my birthday!"

Grandma hugged both of the children. Jeff wasn't sure that he understood either grandmothers or little sisters, but he knew they would have ice cream and cake next, so he didn't worry about it!

Some Questions

1. Do you like to give gifts to others?

2. What makes a gift important to the person who receives it?

Prayer: Dear God, thank You for all the people who love me and all the people whom I love. Thank You for sending Jesus as the greatest gift of all. In Jesus' name. Amen.

 Devotion 24

Let us be concerned for one another, to help one another to show love and to do good.
Hebrews 10:24

How Can You Eat Mushrooms?

The Carson family went out for dinner. It was easy for them to decide where to eat. They all wanted pizza. The waitress came to their table to take their order.

"We'll have two medium pizzas," said the father.

"What will you have on them?" the waitress asked.

"I'd like pineapple," said the mother.

"Oh, no," said Tommy. "Pineapple is for cake and ice cream, not for pizza. I want meatballs."

"Meatballs are for spaghetti," said Lucy. "I'd like mushrooms."

"Yuck," said David, "How can you eat mushrooms? They're a fungus. Do you know what a fungus is? It's what grows in Lucy's ears. I want green peppers."

"My ears don't have fungus," said Lucy.

"All of you be still," said their mother. "The waitress is waiting for us to make up our minds. What do you want, honey?" she asked her husband.

"I was going to say anchovies," said the father, "but in this crowd, I'm not sure."

"That's dead fish with their insides still in them," said Tommy.

"And they still have their heads," said Lucy. "Fish-head pizza."

"We can work this out," said the father. Then to the waitress he said, "Two medium pizzas, all with cheese. One of them will be half anchovies and half mushrooms. The other will be half meatballs and half pineapple and green peppers. That should make everyone happy."

"But maybe there won't be enough of the kind I like," said Lucy.

"Everyone will get at least two pieces of the kind they like," said their mother. "Then maybe you will want to try something different and learn to enjoy something new."

"But it's dumb to eat some of that stuff," said Tommy.

"Look at the menu," said their mother. "See all the different toppings they offer? People like different things because they are different. Even in our family we have a lot of different things we like and don't like. But that's okay. If you get to choose what you want, you have to let others choose what they want."

"Okay," said Lucy, "but I won't eat fish heads."

Some Questions

1. What are some of the things you like (food and otherwise) that others may not like?

2. How can you let other people enjoy something that they like, but you don't?

Prayer: Lord Jesus, help me understand why some people like things I don't like, and help others understand why I like things they don't like. Help me share Your love with all people. Amen.

Devotion 25

Everything you do or say, then, should be done in the name of the Lord Jesus, as you give thanks through Him to God the Father.
Colossians 3:17

He Said a Dirty Word

"Mom! Mom!" Susie cried when her mother came in the house with two large sacks of groceries. "Raymond said a dirty word."

"I did not," Raymond said, defending himself.

"Yes, you did," said Susie.

"Calm down and let me put these bags down. They're heavy," said their mother. "Now, what's the problem?"

"Raymond said a dirty word," repeated Susie.

"What did he say?" their mother asked.

"I'm not supposed to say that word," said Susie.

"What did you say, Raymond?" their mother asked him.

"I didn't say anything that was bad," said Raymond.

"Yes, you did," said Susie. "You said your penis itched."

"What's wrong with that?" asked Raymond.

"That's a dirty word," said his sister.

"No," said their mother. "Penis is not a dirty word. It's a good word for a part of a boy's body."

"But you said we shouldn't say those words about our bodies," said Susie.

"Oh, no," said their mother. "Either I didn't say it right or you misunderstood. I said we shouldn't use dirty words to talk about our bodies. We should use the good words because we know that our bodies are good. God created every part of us, and when He had finished creating us, He said all that He had made was very good."

"Then why are some words dirty?" asked Susie.

"Because they make the body sound bad, or they make

people feel ashamed," said their mother. "I want you to know the good words. Raymond has a penis, and you, Susie, have a vagina. Sometimes we need to talk about our bodies, and I want you to know the good words so you do not have to be ashamed of your body."

"Then why do we cover up those parts of our body when other people are around?" asked Raymond. (He wasn't so sure of these things and had said the word *penis* in the first place to find out what would happen.)

"Because parts of our body are private," said their mother. "We don't cover them to hide them because they're bad. Those parts are personal. Other people should not look at them or touch them. They are a very special part of us, and we keep them private for the one person we will marry—who is also very special to us."

"Did you buy any cookies?" asked Raymond, who had had enough of the conversation.

"I hope you did," said Susie, "because he ate the last one in the box while you were gone."

Some Questions

1. Do you know the good names for all the parts of your body?

2. What questions do you want to ask about your body?

Prayer: Thank You, God, for creating us with beautiful bodies. Help us respect our own bodies and the bodies of others. In Jesus' name. Amen.

Devotion 26

Children, it is your Christian duty to obey
your parents, for this is the right thing to do.
"Respect your father and mother" is the first
commandment that has a promise added: "so
that all may go well with you, and you may
live a long time in the land." Ephesians 6:1–3

You Can't Tell Me What to Do!

Carla and her stepmother had gone to the mall to buy
some new clothes. School would start in a couple weeks,
and Carla had grown a lot during the summer. This was
their first shopping trip together because Carla's father
had gotten married again recently. Carla and her stepmother were still trying to learn to live together.

As they entered the mall, Carla turned toward the
department store that had the kind of clothes she wanted.
Her stepmother turned the other way.

"I need to leave this prescription at the drugstore first,"
she said.

"I'll meet you in the junior department by the jeans,"
said Carla.

"No, you come with me," said her stepmother. "Then
we'll go shopping together."

"You're not my mother," said Carla. "You can't tell me
what to do."

"Okay, since I'm not your mother," said her stepmother, "I'll take you home. Then I'll go shopping."

"But I don't want you to buy the things that I wear,"
said Carla.

"I don't intend to," said her stepmother. "I'll buy things for me to wear."

"But I need clothes for school," said Carla. "You're supposed to get them."

"That's something a mother does," said her stepmother. "I'm your father's wife, and I'm glad that you live with us. I want to do the things that a mother does because I love you and because you're the only daughter I'll ever have. But if I'm going to do the things that a mother does for you, then you must do the things that a daughter does for me."

Carla stood still for a moment, then started walking toward the drugstore. Her stepmother walked with her and left the prescription at the counter. "It will be ready in about an hour," said the pharmacist.

"Sometimes mothers and daughters go shopping and then have lunch," said Carla's stepmother. "Do you think we could do that today?"

"I hope so," said Carla.

Some Questions

1. What does your family need to do to help everyone work together better?

2. How can you help others in your family so they can also help you?

3. How will Jesus' example help you as you work out family problems?

Prayer: Holy Spirit, bless our family. Help us to talk to one another and to listen to one another. In Jesus' name. Amen.

Devotion 27

Wolves and lambs will eat together; lions will eat straw, as cattle do, and snakes will no longer be dangerous. On Zion, My sacred hill, there will be nothing harmful or evil.
Isaiah 65:25

Will My Dog Be in Heaven?

Jason was in his room, crying. The door was shut. The light was out. He heard a knock on the door.

"Who's there?" he asked and hoped that his voice did not sound as if he had been crying.

"Daddy," a voice said. "May I come in?"

"If you want to," said Jason as he sat up on the bed and wiped his nose and eyes with his hand. Dad came into the room. He didn't turn on the light, but he left the door open, and the hall light shone into the room.

"What do you want?" Jason asked.

"I'm sad," Dad said, "so I wanted to talk to you."

"Why are you sad?" asked Jason.

"Because I'm sorry that Ralph is dead," said Jason's father. Ralph was Jason's dog, the only dog he had ever owned. That day while the family was away, Ralph had dug a hole under the fence and run out into the street. A car had hit him and killed him.

"He was my dog," said Jason.

"I know," said his father. "And I know you will miss him most of all. But I loved Ralph too. So I feel sad for you because you miss your dog, and I feel sad because I miss him too."

"Will Ralph be in heaven?" asked Jason.

"I'm glad you asked," said his father. "You know that *we* will be in heaven someday, don't you?"

"I know that," said Jason. "You said that Grandpa went to heaven because Jesus loved him and died for him. You said Grandpa would rise from the dead one day as Jesus did. What about Ralph? Does Jesus love him?"

"Oh, yes," said his dad. "God created your dog."

"Did Jesus die for Ralph's sins?" asked Jason.

"Remember the story of the Garden of Eden?" Dad asked. "People sinned. The animals didn't. But they suffered because we were supposed to take care of them. Because we do wrong things, we don't take care of the animals as we should."

"You didn't answer my question," Jason said.

"As far as we know, animals don't have souls, and Jesus didn't have to die for them. But God promises us joy and happiness in heaven. If Ralph isn't with us, God will help us feel happy that Ralph had a good life and that he didn't have to live in pain after the car hit him."

"I think I still will miss Ralph in heaven," Jason said.

"God will be there," said Dad. "We'll be there. If God loves us enough to give us life with Him, can we trust Him to take care of Ralph?"

"I think so," said Jason.

"So do I."

Some Questions

1. Why do many people like to have pets?

2. Can you love animals? Can they love you?

Prayer: Thank You, God, for our pets, other people's pets, the animals on the farm and in the zoo, and all animals everywhere! In Jesus' name. Amen.

 ## Devotion 28

Don't you know that your body is the temple of the Holy Spirit, who lives in you and who was given to you by God? You do not belong to yourselves but to God; He bought you for a price. So use your bodies for God's glory.
1 Corinthians 6:19–20

We'll Give You Something Else

Andy and his parents were on vacation, driving to a national park. "Do you like my friend Ben?" Andy asked his parents.

"Yes," said his mother. "I enjoy having him at our house."

"I like him," answered Andy's father. "Why do you ask?"

"Because he's my best friend," answered Andy.

"Good," said his father. "Maybe he can go on a vacation with us sometime."

"Did you know that Ben isn't going to smoke cigarettes until he gets out of high school?" asked Andy.

"That's good," answered his mother, "but why just until he gets out of high school?"

"Because his mom and dad said they would give him $1,000 if he doesn't smoke until then. I think that's a good idea, don't you?"

"I think it's a good idea not to smoke," answered his father.

"Would you give me $1,000 if I don't smoke until I'm through high school?" Andy asked.

The parents looked at each other. They were ready for this one.

"No," said his mother, "but we'll give you something else."

"What will you give me?" Andy asked.

"We'll give you lessons on how to make good decisions," said his mother. "We hope you can decide for yourself not to use tobacco."

"I'd rather have the thousand dollars," said Andy.

"I can understand why," said his father. "But you'd spend the thousand dollars, and then it would be gone. If you learn how to make decisions by following Jesus' example, that will last you as long as you live."

"And if you don't smoke," added his mother, "you'll live a lot longer."

"But Ben is learning how to make a decision," Andy persisted. "He decided he wanted the money, so he won't smoke."

"But once he gets the money, he will feel that he can smoke. We want you to learn that smoking is bad for your health, not just while you are in school, but for all of your life. God gives us our bodies and our health. Taking care of our health is a way of thanking Him."

"That's a lot to think about," Andy said.

"You've got on your seat belt, right?" asked his mother.

"Yes."

"Then I think you are learning to make good decisions, for the right reasons."

"When are we going to get there?" asked Andy.

Some Questions

1. What decisions can you make for yourself now?

2. When do you still need your parents to help you make decisions?

   Prayer: Dear God, help me take good care of my body and make decisions that honor You. In Jesus' name. Amen.

 ## Devotion 29

[Jesus said,] "I will be with you always, to the end of the age." Matthew 28:20

Do You Think God Was with Us?

Zach and Aaron were riding their bikes down the sidewalk, talking about the soccer game their team had just won. They saw the traffic light turn green and rode across the intersection without getting off their bikes—and without waiting for the "walk" signal to cross the street.

A car turned left and headed straight for the two boys. The driver slammed on the brakes, and the car skidded to a stop a few inches from Zack and Aaron. The boys froze in fear, and so did the driver. They realized how close they all had been to being part of a terrible accident.

The boys rode on for a short distance, then stopped to rest on a bus stop bench. They were both shaking with fear as they thought about what might have happened.

"Do you think God was with us back there?" Zack finally asked.

"He must have been," Aaron answered. "We could have been dead by now."

"There would have been ambulances and paramedics," said Zack. "And someone would have called our parents."

The thought of their parents receiving such a phone call made the two friends sit in silence for a while.

"Was that a miracle?" asked Zack.

"It might have been," said Aaron. "We always talk at home about God being with us, and my mom and dad always pray that all of us kids will be protected. Maybe God answered their prayers."

"Yeah. My Sunday school teacher says that God is always with us too," said Zack. "Maybe this is what she's talking about."

"But would God have been with us if we would have gotten hurt?" Aaron asked.

"I guess so," said Zack. "Sometimes people do get hit by cars."

"Well, I'm glad He protected us from getting hurt this time. It's good to know God is always with us." They got on their bikes and rode home—carefully.

Some Questions

1. Talk about some times when God has protected you.

2. Do you think God is with people even when bad things happen? Why or why not?

Prayer: Thank You for protecting us, God. Thank You for being with us all the time. In Jesus' name. Amen.

 ## Devotion 30

Mary remembered all these things and thought deeply about them. Luke 2:19

Did He Know He Was God?

The Williams family was driving home on Christmas Eve. They had gone to church to celebrate Jesus' birth. Kaitlyn had been in the Sunday school choir and sang her favorite Christmas song, "Away in a Manger."

"Did He know He was God?" Kaitlyn asked from the backseat.

"Did who know He was God?" her mother asked.

"Jesus," the girl answered. "When He was a little baby in the manger, did He know He was God?"

"I don't know," said her mother. "I never thought about that before."

"He must have known," said Kaitlyn, "because God knows everything."

"But He became a real person," said her father. "He was a little baby just as you were when you were born. You don't remember that, do you?"

"No," she answered. "But I wasn't God."

"You've got a point," said her father.

"But to me it's important that Jesus was really a little human baby who needed His parents and others to take care of Him," Mom said. "Even though He was God, He didn't use His power. He became like us in every way except that He didn't sin. That was so He could die in our place to pay for our sins."

"I know that," said Kaitlyn. "But I'd still like to know if baby Jesus knew He was God."

"I know," said her father. "But maybe that's not an important part of the story. God doesn't tell us every-thing—just what we need to know to get to heaven. Maybe when we're there, He'll fill us in on the rest."

"Okay," said Kaitlyn, "but now let's talk about the pre-sents under the tree. I get to open the big green one with the white ribbons first."

Some Questions

1. Do you have questions that you'd like to ask about how Jesus was born?

2. How would you answer Kaitlyn's question?

Prayer: Thank You, God, for sending Jesus to live with us. Amen.

 ## Devotion 31

Do everything without complaining or arguing, so that you may be innocent and pure as God's perfect children. Philippians 2:14–15a

You Don't Want Me to Have Fun?

Heather came home from school very excited. Her friend Kasi had invited her to a party after school the next day. Kasi had already been to her house, and her mother knew Kasi's mother, so Heather was sure she could go to the party.

"Kasi lives close to the school," explained Heather. "So we can walk home together. There is a crossing guard at the corner." Heather added that because she knew her mother would ask.

"But how will you get home after the party?" asked her mother.

"You can come and get me," Heather said.

"Oh, sweetie, I'd like to," said her mother, "but I have a business meeting after work tomorrow. I've arranged for Mrs. Carter to stay with you, and she doesn't drive."

Heather realized for the first time that she might not get to go to the party. She just *had* to go.

"That's no problem, Mom," she said. "I can walk home, really I can. It's only a mile or something like that."

"No, it would be too dangerous for you to walk home, especially at that time of the evening."

"Maybe I could stay all night at Kasi's house," suggested Heather.

"Kasi's mother has to go to work very early in the morning," said Heather's mother. "She already worries about leaving Heather alone for that time. She wouldn't want to be responsible for another child."

"You don't want me to have any fun," said Heather as

tears started running down her cheeks.

"I want you to have fun," said her mother. "But I also want you to be safe. It would be too dangerous for a girl your age to walk home by herself."

"But I want to go to the party," said Heather, who was sobbing by now.

"I know you do," said her mother, "but I also want you to be safe—so you can have fun for a long time. Kasi's mother and I will plan something special for you and Kasi to do later."

Some Questions

1. How do you feel when you don't get to do what you want to do?

2. Why must parents say no to their children sometimes?

> **Prayer:** Dear God, thank You for parents who protect me when I am in danger. Help me stay away from places where I might get hurt. In Jesus' name. Amen.

 ## Devotion 32

> *I consider that what we suffer at this present time cannot be compared at all with the glory that is going to be revealed to us. Romans 8:18*

Will It Hurt?

Mary sat by herself in the doctor's waiting room. Her parents were talking to the doctor—about her. For several days she had felt a pain in her side. She told her mother where she hurt, and her parents decided to take her to see the doctor. She liked her doctor, but she didn't like to undress away from home and have the doctor poke on her body. But the doctor explained that she must look for the pain and that she needed Mary to help her find it.

"We have some good news and some bad news," her father said when they came out of the doctor's office. "The good news is that you are a healthy kid."

"Then why do I hurt?" asked Mary.

"That's the bad news," said her father. "You have a hernia and will have to have surgery next week."

"No!" said Mary. "I know what surgery is. They use a knife and cut you. I don't want surgery!"

Mary's mother sat down beside her and held her hand.

"We won't let anyone harm you," she said. "Dr. Kendell is your friend. She has another doctor who works with her who will do the operation."

"But will it hurt?" Mary asked.

"Yes, it will hurt some," said her mother, "but you will be put to sleep before the operation so you won't feel the pain then. After that it will be sore for a few days."

"But I don't want to hurt," said Mary.

"That's why you need to have surgery," said her father, who was now sitting on the other side of her. "You have a pain now. It will get worse until we do something about it. We don't want you to hurt any more than you do now."

"You will have some pain for a while because of the operation," said her mother, "but it will be a lot less pain than you would have if you didn't have the surgery."

Mary sat without saying anything. She was still scared.

"One more thing," said her father. "Remember that at church every Sunday we all pray for people who are sick and who need help. We will put your name on that prayer list, and all the people in church will pray for you—just as you have prayed for others. And Mom and I will be right there with you."

"Can I take my teddy bear with me to the hospital?" Mary asked.

Some Questions

1. Can you think of things that hurt for a little but that help you later?

2. How does God help you when you have a problem?

3. Do you know someone for whom you should pray right now?

Prayer: Dear Jesus, please be with me when I hurt. Please help_____also. Amen.

 ## Devotion 33

Do not get drunk with wine, which will only ruin you; instead, be filled with the Spirit.
Ephesians 5:18

She's Drunk Again

"Mom," Ann yelled after she had hung up the phone, "can Heather come over and spend the night with me?"

"It's too late to plan for company," her mother said. "We've already had dinner."

"That's okay," said Ann. "We'll find something for Heather to eat in the refrigerator."

"I'll have to talk to Heather's mother first," said Mom.

"No, please don't call her," said Ann. "It will be okay."

"But Heather can't just come over without her mother knowing."

"Her mom's drunk again," said Ann.

Ann and her mother were quiet for a while. They had talked about this before. They knew that Heather's mother had a drinking problem. They also knew that Heather's father traveled a lot. Heather was always afraid to go home when her father was gone because her mother drank more then.

"How can we help Heather?" Ann's mother asked.

"I don't know," said Ann. "We prayed about it just as you said we should. But her mother still gets drunk."

"You had a good idea. We can invite her to spend the night with us," said Ann's mother. "I'll drive over to pick Heather up. I know her mother will let her come."

"But will she have to go back tomorrow?" asked Ann.

"Yes, after school," said her mother. "I'll leave a note so her mother knows we are taking her to school. I'm going to talk to the counselor at school and ask her to call Heather's father."

"Will that get Heather into trouble?" asked Ann.

"No," said her mother. "That's another way to help Heather. We'll have to think of more ways too."

Some Questions

1. Does your family have problems become of the misuse of alcohol?

2. Do you know other families that have troubles because someone drinks too much alcohol?

3. What can you do to help your friends who have problems because someone in their family drinks too much alcohol or uses drugs?

Prayer: Dear God, please help all children who live in homes where someone gets drunk. Protect the children and give the adults a way to get help through Jesus Christ. Amen.

 ## Devotion 34

In the same way the Spirit also comes to help us, weak as we are. For we do not know how we ought to pray; the Spirit Himself pleads with God for us in groans that words cannot express. Romans 8:26

I Don't Know What to Pray For

Mrs. Barret's Sunday school class was talking about prayer. They had read a story Jesus told about a woman who demanded that a neighbor help her. Jesus said that His followers should pray to God in the same way.

"When do you pray?" Mrs. Barret asked.

"I pray before I go to sleep," said Carla.

"We always pray before and after we eat," said Clark.

"I pray in church," said Libby.

"My family always prays in the car when we go on a trip," said Kara.

Mrs. Barret noticed that Eric was listening but had not said anything. She said, "Eric, do you want to tell us when you pray?"

"I don't know how to pray," he said.

The other students were surprised. "Eric," Clark reminded him, "we pray in class and talk about prayer all the time."

"But I don't know what to pray for," said Eric.

"Just ask for whatever you want," said Clark.

"Maybe we should ask Eric to explain what he means," said Mrs. Barret.

"My grandmother is very sick," Eric said. "The doctors said that she's going to die real soon. We used to pray that she would get well."

"That's good," said Mrs. Barret. "We'll pray for her here too, and I'll ask the pastor to pray for her in church today."

"But that's not all," said Eric. "The doctors said that even if she lives longer, she will not get well. She will hurt a lot and have to live in a nursing home. I don't know if I should pray that she get well or pray that she could die and go to heaven."

All of the students were quiet. Mrs. Barret could see that they understood Eric's problem.

"I'm glad that you know that she can die and go to heaven because Jesus is her Savior," said Mrs. Barret. "I understand why you wonder how you should pray. But let's think about it. When we pray, we are not telling God what to do. God knows more than we do, and He loves us. When we pray, we are asking for His help. We even ask Him to help us understand things that are difficult. We can pray for your grandmother by asking God to be with her and bless her. God will know the best way to help her."

"Could we pray that now?" Eric asked.

Some Questions

1. What are some of the things that you pray about?

2. Do you always know what to say to God?

3. Why does God have to answer some of our prayers by saying no?

Prayer: Our Father in heaven, thank You for listening to our prayers. Please give us what is best for ourselves and others. In Jesus' name. Amen.

 ## Devotion 35

If we are not faithful, He [Jesus] remains faithful, because He cannot be false to Himself. 2 Timothy 2:13

He Doesn't Believe in Jesus Anymore

Randy looked forward to spending summer vacation with his grandparents. He liked to do lots of things at their house, but most of all he liked to be with his cousin Ryan, who lived a block away. Ryan was 10 years older than Randy, but they always had fun.

This year Randy was disappointed. Ryan was not with their grandparents at the airport.

"Didn't he know I was coming?" Randy asked.

"Yes, he knew," said their grandmother, "but he is at a sports camp for two weeks."

"Then I won't get to see him at all," said Randy.

"Ryan will be home for the weekend," explained his grandfather. "I'm sure that you'll see him then."

Randy did other things that were sort of fun, but he looked forward to Saturday. On Saturday morning Ryan phoned to talk to Randy. He explained that he had lots of things to do, but he would see his cousin on Sunday.

Randy knew that his family always went to church together, so he looked forward to sitting with his older cousin. But the next day his uncle and aunt were at church and Ryan wasn't. After church they all went to his grandparents' house for dinner. Ryan came just as they sat down to eat. Randy noticed that Ryan didn't join in saying the prayer. The two cousins went out for a walk, then Ryan had to leave for camp again.

That evening Randy's grandmother came to his room and noticed that he was crying. "What's the matter?" she asked.

"Do you know that Ryan doesn't believe in Jesus any-more?" Randy said. "That's what he told me when I asked why he wasn't in church and why he didn't pray."

"I know he's been having some problems," said Grandmother. "I think he's angry at God."

"But he said he doesn't even *believe* in God," said Randy.

"That makes me sad," said their grandmother, "but I am glad that God still loves Ryan."

"But God can't love Ryan, if Ryan doesn't love God," Randy said.

"Yes, He can," said his grandmother. "God won't ever stop loving us."

"How do you know?"

"Think about what God did for us," said his grandmother. "He let His Son, Jesus, live for us and die for us. That's a big deal. If God loves us that much, nothing can stop Him from loving us. We need to help Ryan know that God still loves him."

"But can Ryan still go to heaven?" asked Randy.

"You and I don't decide who goes to heaven," said Grandmother. "But we know that God wants all of us to be in heaven with Him. God will not give up on Ryan."

"And I won't either," said Randy. "I'll pray for him every night."

"Good," said Grandmother. "I've been praying for him every day, and I pray for you too."

Some Questions

1. Do you know some people who do not believe in Jesus? What can you do for them?

2. How does God keep your faith strong?

Prayer: Holy Spirit, thank You for making me God's child in my Baptism and for teaching me about Jesus. Help my faith grow stronger and stronger as I get older. Amen.

Devotion 36

*Dear friends, let us love one another, because
love comes from God. Whoever loves is a
child of God and knows God.* 1 John 4:7

But I Don't Want a Baby Sister

Cory and Matt knew something was going on at their
house. For two weeks they had heard their parents talking in whispers. When they tried to sneak up close to
hear what their mother and father were talking about,
their parents would change the subject.

"Why are you and Dad always whispering about
things?" Cory asked his mother.

"You'll find out soon enough," she answered with a
smile.

"You tell us that we have to tell you about the things
we are doing," Matt told his father. "Why don't you tell
us what's going on?"

"We'll tell you when we're sure," his father answered.

Finally, at dinner one evening, Mom said, "We have a
big surprise for you."

"Are we going to get to go on a vacation to the moun-
tains?" asked Matt.

"It better not be that we are going to move," said Cory,
"because I want to stay here."

"No, the surprise is better than anything like that," Dad
laughed.

"Then tell us," said Cory.

"We're going to have a baby," said Mom. "Maybe you

will finally have a sister."

"But I don't want a baby sister," said Matt.

"And I don't want another brother either," said Cory.

"But it will be fun to have a baby in the house again," said their mother. "You two are old enough now to enjoy a baby."

"Jimmy's family has a little baby," said Cory. "He pukes and cries and stinks. That's not fun."

"I guess you did all those things too," said Dad, "but we had fun with you then just as we do now. The baby will be someone for you to love."

"But you won't have as much time for us," said Matt, "because you'll have to take care of the baby."

"But we'll love you just as much," said Mom.

"No, you won't," said Matt, "because you will have to divide your love among three kids instead of two."

"But it doesn't work that way," said Dad. "It's true that we'll have one more person to love, but remember that we'll also have one more person to love us. Instead of having less love, we'll have more. It's God's love in us that helps our love grow and grow."

"The baby, whether it's a boy or a girl, will be glad to have two big brothers like you," said their mother. "Once you see the baby and hold it, you will see how a baby can love you. That will make you happy."

"But she will get into our things and mess up our room," said Cory.

"I think that's already been done," said his father.

Some Questions

1. What are the advantages and disadvantages of being

the only child? of having a brother or sister? of having more brothers and sisters?

2. How can you share God's love with a younger brother or sister? with an older one?

Prayer: Dear God, thank You for our family. Help us share the blessings of our family with others. In Jesus' name. Amen.

 ## Devotion 37

Be tolerant with one another and forgive one another whenever any of you has a complaint against someone else. You must forgive one another just as the Lord has forgiven you.
Colossians 3:13

I Don't Want to Choose between You

Jenny's father watched as she talked to her mother on the phone. He saw tears swelling up in her eyes and then running down her face. She talked very quietly, hung up the phone, and ran to her room. Her father waited for a while, then knocked on her door.

"May I come in, sweetie?" he asked.

"If you want to," Jenny replied.

Jenny was holding her stuffed rabbit and looking out the window. Her father sat down on the floor near her.

"Can you tell me what's wrong?" he asked.

"Yes," she sobbed. "Mom said that I need to decide whether I will be with you or her on Saturday. I don't want to choose between you."

Saturday was Jenny's birthday—the first since her parents' divorce. Her father thought about the long, and sometimes angry, discussion that he and Jenny's mother had had about the birthday. They finally agreed that Jenny should make the choice about which parent she would be with on her special day. Now he realized that was the best solution for them but not for Jenny.

"I want to be with both of you," said Jenny. "I don't want to be with Mom and think that you are lonely without me, and I don't want to be with you and know that she isn't happy. I wish I didn't have a birthday."

"I'm sorry, Jenny," said Dad. "Your mother and I made a mistake. You shouldn't have to pick between us. We don't want to put our problems on you. Your mother and I love you, and we still love Jesus. He forgives us. Jenny, will you forgive us too for our mistakes?"

"Yes," said Jenny as she wiped away tears. "But that doesn't help me decide what to do on my birthday. May I ask Peggy if I can go to her house and not be with either one of you?"

"That's one solution," said her father. "But I have another. You spend the day with your mother and have a good time. I will be happy if I know you are glad to be with your mother."

"But then I'll feel bad because you are alone," said Jenny.

"You won't have to feel bad," said her father, "because next year you will spend your birthday with me. If I get lonely for you, I'll think about what we will do on your birthday a year from now. I'll have time to plan a very special day."

"Will that be okay with Mom?" asked Jenny.

"I think it will," said her father. "You can call her now and tell her about the plan. I think she'll like it."

Some Questions

1. Do you have to make choices between your parents if they are divorced or even if they're not divorced?

2. What are some of the ways you can show both of your parents that you love them?

3. Have you thanked God and your parents if they are not divorced?

Prayer: Dear Jesus, we know You love us. Forgive us when we hurt one another and help us to share Your love and forgiveness. Amen.

 ## Devotion 38

So God created human beings, making them to be like Himself. He created them male and female, blessed them, and said, "Have many children, so that your descendants will live all over the earth and bring it under their control." Genesis 1:27–28

What's Love Got to Do with It?

"How was school today?" Mark's mother asked as he looked through the refrigerator for an apple.

"Okay," Mark answered. "I learned about sex."

"I suppose I'd feel better if I knew who taught the lesson," said his mother.

"The teacher did," Mark answered as he sliced the apple.

"And what did the teacher have to say?" his mother asked.

"Most of the stuff I already knew," he answered. "I knew about sperm and eggs and sexual intercourse because you and Dad already told me some of those things and I figured some of it out by myself."

"Maybe it's good for you to get a second opinion on the things we have taught you," said Mom. "And it's also a good idea to check out things you figured out by yourself."

"There's one thing I'd like to know," Mark said.

"What's that?" his mother asked.

"What's love got to do with it?" Mark asked. "You and Dad explained things by talking about making love. The teacher talked about sex. Is that the same thing?"

"Sometimes, but not always," said his mother. "Some people use sex without loving each other. There are also many ways to love other people without sex. But love and sex go together for a husband and wife in a very special way."

"How?" Mark asked.

"When God made the first man and woman, He gave them the ability to keep on making more people. He made one a male—he has the seed—and He made the other one a female—she has the egg. They need each other to have children. That's the sex part."

"Okay, but what about the love part?"

"When God made us, He used His power to create, but

He also used love," explained Mark's mother. "He made a plan that every baby born would be loved. If we all followed His plan, it would work this way: Every baby born would have a father who knows how to love a woman and a mother who knows how to love a man. Then their baby would be born, not just because they had sex, but because they loved each other."

"That sounds like a good plan," said Mark.

"Your father and I love each other in a special way, and that's why we have you," said his mother. "Each of us loves you in a different way, so you are growing up with the love from a father and from a mother."

"But Jimmy has never even seen his dad," said Mark. "And Gary only sees his mother during the summer and sometimes at Christmas."

"I know," said his mother. "Sometimes we don't follow God's plan. Sometimes a mother and father cannot love each other anymore. But they can still love their children."

"It's hard to love someone you don't even know," said Mark.

"That's true," said his mother. "Our human love is never perfect. Even though your father and I will never get a divorce, we may not always love you the way we want to. That's why God sent Jesus to be our Savior. When our kind of love fails, we need to know that His love will forgive us and help us."

"Do you think my teacher knows about that?" asked Mark.

"I hope she does," said his mother.

Some Questions

1. Do you have questions that you would like to ask about sex?

2. Think about a married couple who love each other in a good way. What can you learn from them?

3. Do you know married people who do not show love for each other? What can you learn from them?

Prayer: Thank You, Father in heaven, for giving love to me and to my family. Help us love one another. Help me to learn how to love another person as a husband or wife when I grow up. In Jesus' name. Amen.

Devotion 39

Our life is cut short by Your anger; it fades away like a whisper. Seventy years is all we have—eighty years, if we are strong; yet all they bring us is trouble and sorrow; life is soon over, and we are gone. Teach us how short our life is, so that we may become wise.
Psalm 90:9–10, 12

Share Your Memories with Someone

Cindy and Rick were excited about going to the airport to pick up their dad. He'd left suddenly on Friday to visit his Uncle Harold. Now it was Sunday evening, and their father's plane was on time.

"I hope you haven't eaten dinner," Dad said as they got in the car.

"I figured you wouldn't like the airplane food," said their mother, "so I have sandwiches ready for us."

"We'll have the sandwiches tomorrow," said Dad. "Tonight Uncle Harold is taking us to dinner." Cindy and Rick were surprised when their father drove into the parking lot of a fancy restaurant.

"I don't think we're dressed right to eat here," Mom said.

"Don't worry," said their father. "Uncle Harold would love this." When they were seated, their father told them they could order anything they wanted. Then he ordered appetizers for everyone.

"Okay, I suppose I could let the kids ask," said Mom, "but what is going on? Why are you so excited about Uncle Harold? I've never met him, and I don't think the kids have even heard of him."

"I'm glad you asked," Dad said, "because Uncle Harold is paying for this dinner so I can explain something to you for him."

"What is it?" asked Rick. "Did he give you lots of money?"

"Not lots," said their father. "Enough to pay for this dinner and to leave a big tip. But he gave us something more important than money."

"Tell us," said Cindy. She was so excited that she'd forgotten what she had ordered.

"This is the story," said Dad. "I've only seen Uncle Harold two or three times in my life. When he was young, he went to work for the government in the foreign service. We hardly ever heard from him. Once in a while my dad, Uncle Harold's brother, would get a Christmas card from him. It would always come from some place in Asia or Africa. When I was a teenager, I dreamed of growing up and being like Uncle Harold, even though I didn't know him. Then I fell in love with your mother, got married, had you kids, bought a house with a big mortgage, and forgot about Uncle Harold."

"You sound as if you think you might have missed having more adventure in your life," said Mom.

"No, that's the point," explained their father. "When Uncle Harold phoned me last week and said he was sending a plane ticket for me to visit him, I had no idea what he wanted. I hadn't seen him in more than 25 years. When I got there, he told me he has cancer and will die in a couple months."

"How sad," said their mother.

"That's not the worst part," said their father. "He feels he has wasted his life. No one is with him."

"But he must have done a lot of neat things," said Rick.

"Oh, he has," Dad said. "But he told me he has no one to share his memories with. He did all those exciting things with people he didn't even know well. They were all business associates. He has no friends and no family. Last year, he decided he would give all his money to me because I had a wife and children, but he has spent most of his money on medical bills in the last six months."

"So why did he want to see you?" asked their mother.

"He wanted me to do something kind of strange—like pulling into this expensive restaurant—so all of you would remember it," explained Dad. "He wanted me to tell you that the most important thing in life is to have memories that you share with others who love you."

"This *is* kind of strange," said Cindy.

"I think I'll always remember it," said Rick.

"I don't think I agree with your uncle that sharing memories is the most important thing in life. Is there anything we can do for him?" asked Mom.

"I tried," said Dad. "Like all my family, Uncle Harold grew up going to church and believing in Jesus. But he had forgotten that part of his life. We talked about it. I told him that was a memory that we could still share— with each other and with Jesus. He liked that idea."

"Can we write him a letter and tell him about this dinner?" asked Rick.

"I think that's a good idea," said Dad as the waitress came with a big tray of nachos and chicken wings. "And we'll tell Uncle Harold we're praying for him too."

Some Questions

1. Do you already have memories of things that you have done that you like to talk about with others?

2. What are you doing now that will give you good memories when you are older?

3. Are you doing anything that will give you bad memories? How will Jesus help you with these memories?

Prayer: Dear Jesus, be a part of my life now so when I am old I can remember that You always have been with me—and always will be. Amen.

Devotion 40

*Do not conform yourselves to the standards
of this world, but let God transform you
inwardly by a complete change of your mind.*
Romans 12:2

It's Pure Pressure

Glenda was busy writing an assignment at school. The
teacher had asked the class to write a theme called, "I Go
to School Because ..."

At first Glenda couldn't think of anything to write. She
went to school because everyone went to school. She
didn't have a choice. Then she thought about what it
would be like not to go to school. She started writing.

Glenda wrote some of the things she knew her teacher
expected: I go to school to learn things. I go to school to
play with my friends. I go to school because my parents
want me to.

As she looked over the things she had written, Glenda
realized that her friends would tease her if she didn't go
to school. They would call her a dumb bunny. She wrote,
"I go to school because of pure pressure."

Mrs. Fisher walked by the students' desks as the class
was busy writing. When she came to Glenda's desk, she
stopped and read what she had written.

"That's very good," said the teacher. "You have neat
handwriting, Glenda. What do you mean by *pure pressure?*"

"Pressure is when someone makes you do something,"
said Glenda.

"And pure?" asked the teacher.

"Pure means that's all it is. My blouse is pure cotton," said Glenda.

"You are a good student and know how to use words," said the teacher. "Have you heard anyone talk about pure pressure?"

"My parents do," said Glenda.

"I thought so," said Mrs. Fisher. "You have the wrong word. You mean *peer* pressure. A peer is another person like you. The other children in this class are your peers. When you do things to please them, it is because of peer pressure."

Glenda erased the word she had written. She thought about the words *pure pressure* and *peer pressure.* She thought about what the other kids would say if they thought she was different than them. She thought about how she wanted to make them like her.

Glenda looked at her paper. She saw the blank place where she had erased. She wrote *pure* in that space again.

Some Questions

1. Do you agree with Glenda that *peer* pressure could be called *pure* pressure?

2. Whom do you need to please most—your friends, your parents, yourself, your teacher, God?

Prayer: Dear Jesus, thank You for being my Friend. Help me follow You and others who also follow You. Amen.

Devotion 41

Even a child shows what he is by what he
does; you can tell if he is honest and good.
Proverbs 20:11

Your Grandson Is Your Best Heart Medicine

Mr. Lambert was waiting in his doctor's office after
he'd had a lot of tests. He was worried. On his last visit
the doctor had told him his blood pressure was too high.

"Good news for you, Marv," said the doctor as he
walked into the room. "Your blood pressure is down. We
still have to watch it, but you're doing a lot better."

"That's a relief," Mr. Lambert said. "I've been watching my diet."

"What did you do at work this morning?" asked the
doctor.

"Since I had to come in here at noon, I took the whole
day off," said Mr. Lambert. "My 4-year-old grandson
spent the morning with us."

"What did you do?" asked the doctor.

"Ian set the agenda," answered the grandfather. "He
has lots of special routines that he likes to do at our
house—and they all involve me."

"What did he want to do today?"

"He has this thing about hiding," said Mr. Lambert, "so
I put a blanket over the piano, and we crawled under it
together. He learned that if we yell under there, the piano
makes echoes. We had quite a music lesson as we yelled
at different pitches."

"How long did this go on?"

"I never look at my watch when Ian is around," the grandfather answered. "I'm sure we were under the piano for more than half an hour."

"I was going to give you a prescription," said the doctor. "Instead I'm going to refer you to someone else."

"That doesn't sound good," said Mr. Lambert. "I thought you were pleased with my tests."

"I am," said the doctor. "That's why I'm referring you to Ian for further treatment. He's the only one I've heard of who can get you to take time off from work. And I'm sure he's the only one who can get you to spend half an hour yelling under a piano. He's the best heart medicine you have."

Some Questions

1. Why was Ian good medicine for Mr. Lambert?

2. Do children make some older people happy and relaxed? Do they make some older people nervous?

3. Do you know older people who need you? How can you help them?

Prayer: Dear God, thank You for the people who help me. Show me how to be good medicine for the people I love. In Jesus' name. Amen.

 ## Devotion 42

God looked at everything He had made, and He was very pleased. Genesis 1:31a

My Ears Stick Out

Kevin was standing in the bathroom looking in the mirror when his dad came in to brush his teeth.

"What are you doing, Son?" Dad asked. "Checking to see if you are all there?"

"The kids at school tease me," said Kevin, " 'cause my ears stick out."

"I think they're cute," said his father.

"No, they're not! They're ugly," said Kevin. "Besides I don't want to be *cute*."

"When I was your age, my ears were exactly like yours," said his father. "Come on. I'll show you a picture."

The two went into the family room and looked at a photo album. Dad turned several pages.

"Look at that," he said, "your father at age 9. Looks exactly like you. And I remember that I once complained about my ears sticking out. You know what my mother told me?"

"What?" asked Kevin.

"She said, 'Would you rather have ears that stick in or up or down? Ears are supposed to stick out.' That worked for me," said Dad.

"But the kids tease me," complained Kevin.

"Well, some kids will," said Dad. "They'll tease anyone who will get upset about it. Do you tease kids about anything?"

"Only if they do it first," said Kevin.

"If you don't pay any attention, the first tease will also be the last," said Dad. "Now let's go find your mother and tell her how pretty she is. That's more fun than trying to find something wrong with people."

Some Questions

1. Do you worry about how you look?

2. How can you get rid of that problem?

3. Do you make other people feel good or bad about how they look?

Prayer: Dear God, thank You for making me the way I am. Forgive me when I hurt others. Help me like other people the way they are. In Jesus' name. Amen.

 ## Devotion 43

And the Lord will rescue me from all evil and take me safely into His heavenly Kingdom. To Him be glory forever and ever! Amen. 2 Timothy 4:18

My Brother Is in Big Trouble

Three friends sat on the school bus together. Ben was the last one to get on the bus.

"Boy, is my brother in big trouble," he said as he sat down.

"What did he do?" Jason asked.

"I'm not sure," answered Ben. "No one's talking at my house now. But a lot went on last night."

"Tell us," said Aaron.

"Jake got to take the car last night," explained Ben. "He's only had his driver's license for a couple of months, and Dad won't let him take the car by himself very often. But Jake said this was important and that he'd be home by nine o'clock. I had to go to bed at nine, and Jake wasn't home yet. I could tell my dad was mad."

"Well, what happened?" asked Jason.

"I didn't go to sleep," Ben continued. "I heard the phone ring, and I could tell that it was the police. At first Dad sounded scared, then he found out that Jake wasn't hurt or anything. Then he got mad again. He took our other car to go get him."

"Where was Jake?" asked Aaron.

"I don't know," said Ben. "And I could tell this morning that I'd better not ask any questions. But I listened when Dad brought Jake home. He'd dented a fender or something like that. He drove the car home, so it's not too bad. But Jake had some other kids in the car, and they had beer."

"Wow!" said Aaron. "So he's in trouble with the police!"

"I suppose so," said Ben. "But his biggest problem is with Mom and Dad. He's going to be grounded until I'm old enough to drive!"

"Why do teenagers do such stupid things?" asked Jason. "Everybody knows you're not supposed to drink and drive."

"Not all teenagers are stupid," said Aaron.

"Most of them are," said Jason. "They use drugs and dress weird and join gangs. That's dumb. I'm not going to do things like that when I get older."

"My brother doesn't do those things," said Aaron, "and he's a teenager."

"And Jake never got in such big trouble before," said Ben. "I heard him say he didn't drink any beer, but my dad said the driver is responsible."

"What do you think will happen to him?" asked Aaron.

"I'll find out and tell you tomorrow," said Ben.

Some Questions

1. Name some teenagers who live the way you want to live when you are that age.

2. Now name some that live the way you won't want to live.

Prayer: Holy Spirit, help me follow good examples and help me be a good example. In Jesus' name. Amen.

 ## Devotion 44

If you get more stubborn every time you are corrected, one day you will be crushed and never recover. Proverbs 29:1

I Won't Do It!

"I won't do it!" Jacob yelled at his mother. "And you can't make me!"

His mother had told him to take out the garbage. Jacob refused because it wasn't his turn. It was his older brother's turn, but his brother was away from home on a class trip.

"No, I can't make you take out the garbage because that would be more work than doing it myself," said his mother. "But until the garbage is out, you will not watch TV, you will not have dinner, and you won't leave the house."

"Then I'll go live with my daddy," said Jacob. His parents were divorced, and his father lived in another state.

"No, you're living with me," said his mother. "If you did live with your father, he would have chores for you to do too. Obviously we don't agree on everything, but we both agree that you need to be responsible for some chores."

"But it's Randy's turn," said Jacob. "And I won't do it!"

"Then go to your room," said his mother.

Jacob went into his room and slammed the door shut. He could hear the TV and knew that his sister was watching cartoons. He remembered that his friend Joey was coming over to play ball after supper. Speaking of supper, he thought he smelled lasagna. His mother made great lasagna.

But she wasn't being fair. If Randy wasn't home, she should take out the garbage just as ... Then Jacob thought of something. Since his dad didn't live at home, Mom had to do the work that she always did plus most of the chores that Dad had done. Was that fair?

Jacob didn't care about missing TV. But he thought about dinner and Joey coming over. He took the garbage out and came back into the kitchen.

"Sorry, Mom," Jacob said. "What's for dinner?"

Some Questions

1. Tell about a time when you felt you were treated unfairly.

2. Do you think things will always be fair in life? What can your family do when someone feels he or she is being treated unfairly?

   Prayer: Dear Jesus, thank You for thinking about me and what I need. Help me think about others and what they need. Amen.

 ## Devotion 45

If the first piece of bread is given to God, then the whole loaf is His also; and if the roots of a tree are offered to God, the branches are His also. Romans 11:16

How Much Do You Get for an Allowance?

Ben, Aaron, and Jason were on the bus riding home from school. They would get off at the next stop.

"Hey, the bus is 10 minutes early today," said Jason. "Let's stop at the store and get something to eat. I'm hungry."

"Good idea," said Aaron, "but I'm broke."

"You're broke?" said Ben. "You get more allowance than anyone I know. You've got some money in your pocket 'cause I saw it."

"How much do you get?" asked Jason.

"I get 15 bucks a week," said Aaron.

"Wow!" said Jason. "I only get $7."

"You think that's bad," said Ben. "I only get $5. But sometimes I work for my grandpa and make a little more. If I got $15 a week, I'd think I was rich."

"That all depends on what you have to buy with it," said Aaron.

"What do you mean?" asked Ben.

"Mom and Dad give me my allowance on Saturday," said Aaron. "First, I take out a dollar and a half for church, then I put 2 bucks into some kind of mutual fund account they opened for me."

"That still leaves $12.50 for you to spend," said Ben.

"You mean $11.50," said Aaron. "Plus I have to pay for my lunch out of my allowance. Your mothers give you lunch money every day. The money left in my pocket is for lunch for the rest of the week."

"If I had money, I'd spend it now and worry about lunch later," said Ben.

"I did that once and went hungry," said Aaron. "When I asked Mom for extra money, she said she and Dad gave me a big allowance so I'd learn how to manage money. Going without lunch once was enough. Never again!"

"Well, come along with us to the store anyway," said Jason.

"Okay," said Aaron, "if you'll let me smell whatever you eat."

Some Questions

1. How much experience do you have at managing money?

2. Are you learning how to give an offering at church? to save money? to spend money wisely?

Prayer: Thank You, God, for all the things that I have. Help me to remember that they all come from You. In Jesus' name. Amen.

 ## Devotion 46

This is what love is: it is not that we have loved God, but that He loved us and sent His Son to be the means by which our sins are forgiven. 1 John 4:10

No One Else Wants It

Chloe had finished her music lesson. She knew that in a few minutes another student would be coming in for a lesson. She also knew that Miss Melba had to get ready for the other student. But she stood quietly by the door.

"Did you forget something, Chloe?" Miss Melba asked.

Chloe came back to the teacher's desk. She reached into her pocket and pulled out a pencil holder. She had made it herself from a frozen juice can. She had colored some macaroni shells with crayons and pasted them on the can.

"Would you like to have this, Miss Melba?" asked Chloe. "No one else wants it. My mother says she doesn't need a pencil holder. My other teacher says she already has too many pencil holders."

"Chloe, I'd love to have that pencil holder," said Miss Melba. "If you would like to give it to me, I'll use it on my desk at home."

Chloe gave her music teacher the gift and a little hug and ran from the classroom.

Years later, Miss Melba still has the pencil holder made from a juice can covered with macaroni shells. It is one of her most treasured gifts from her years of teaching.

Some Questions

1. Why would someone refuse to accept a gift?

2. What makes a gift valuable?

Prayer: Lord Jesus, as You gave Yourself as a gift to us, help us give and receive gifts as a way of loving one another. Amen.

Devotion 47

A wise son makes his father proud of him; a foolish one brings his mother grief.
Proverbs 10:1b

He Had a Gun—a Real Gun

"Daddy, if I tell you something, will you get mad at me?" Patrick asked.

Patrick's father turned the TV down. He wondered if questions like that made men's hair turn gray. But, he remembered, some single men his age were also getting gray hair so that must not be the reason.

"I'll try to keep cool," said Patrick's dad, "but I'd better hear the story first."

"I was over at Cory's house after school today," Patrick said. "Mom said I could go."

"I can handle that," said his father.

"A couple other kids from our class were there too," said Patrick. "Cory's mom said she would go get some pizza if we would be good while she was gone."

"I'm still with you," said Dad, relaxing a bit.

"As soon as she was gone, Cory took us into his parents' bedroom," said Patrick. "He reached behind some big books on a shelf and pulled out a gun. He had a gun—a *real gun*."

"What happened?" asked Dad, no longer relaxed.

"Cory told us he knew his dad had a gun, so when his parents were both gone once, he looked for it until he found it. He said it was loaded too. He showed us the bullets."

"What did you do?" asked Dad.

"Well, I wanted to hold the gun like the other guys did," said Patrick. "But I remembered how you and Mom told me not to play with guns so I went to the bathroom until I heard Cory's mom come home."

"You did a wise thing," said Dad.

"Cory said I was a chicken," said Patrick.

"No, Son, you were a brave person," said Dad. "A chicken does stupid things because other people do stupid things. A brave person says no when others do wrong things."

"You're not mad at me?" Patrick asked.

"Not only am I not mad at you," said Dad, "I'm proud

of you. You were able to make a decision for yourself, and you made a good one."

"Can I still go to Cory's house?" Patrick asked.

"Yes, as long as you know when to leave," said Dad. "And I think you have proven that today."

Some Questions

1. What should you do when you are with others who do something dangerous?

2. Do you prove you are brave when you do something dangerous?

Prayer: Dear God, protect me from danger and help me know how to avoid danger. In Jesus' name. Amen.

Devotion 48

Be happy with those who are happy, weep with those who weep. Have the same concern for everyone. Do not be proud, but accept humble duties. Do not think of yourselves as wise. Romans 12:15–16

He Let Me Win

Melissa had spent Sunday afternoon with her grandparents. Now she was riding home with her mother.

"Did you have a good time with Grandma and Grandpa?" Mom asked.

"Sort of," Melissa answered. "Grandma let me help her

put frosting on a cake, and I got to lick the pan."

"That sounds like fun," Mom said. "What did you and Grandpa do?"

"He asked me to play checkers with him," said Melissa.

"Who won?"

"I did," Melissa answered. "But Grandpa let me win."

"Why do you think he let you win?" Mom asked.

" 'Cause I've played with him before, and I know he can play better than that," Melissa explained. "He let me take two of his kings, and he didn't get any of mine for it."

"Maybe he let you win because he wants you to be happy," said her mother.

"No, there was a football game on TV," said Melissa. "I think he was in a hurry to get our game over so he could watch it."

"Maybe so," said Mom. "I tell you what. Next time ask him if he wants to play with you first and then watch the game, or watch the game first and then play with you."

"That might work," said Melissa.

Some Questions

1. Why do you like to win a game?

2. Is it fair to cheat to win? to lose?

Prayer: Lord Jesus, help me understand other people and treat them in a loving way, just as You love me. Amen.

 **Devotion 49**

Let us not give up the habit of meeting together, as some are doing. Instead, let us encourage one another all the more, since you see that the Day of the Lord is coming nearer. Hebrews 10:25

We Have to Go to Church

Rick was talking to Matt on the phone. Rick's mother heard one end of the conversation and realized that Rick's friend had invited him to go on a Sunday morning hike.

"I can't go," said Rick, " 'cause we have to go to church on Sunday morning."

The conversation continued for a while, and Rick hung up the phone.

"I am proud of you for telling Matt that you were going to church," said his mother.

"I knew I might as well," said Rick. "You would have said no if I had asked you if I could go."

"You're right," said his mother, "but it was better that you made the decision for yourself instead of asking me. You showed you were responsible."

"What if I would have said that I wanted to go on the hike?" asked Rick.

"We would have discussed it," said Mom.

"What would we have talked about?"

"You said that we *had* to go to church," said his mother. "I probably would have asked if you wanted to go to church."

"Does it make any difference?" asked Rick. "You're the one who decides that we go to church."

"Yes, it makes a big difference," said Mom. "It's my job to make the decisions now. But remember that I go because I want to, not because someone makes me."

"Your mother doesn't go to church," Rick said.

"I know, but I do," said his mother. "Some day you will be old enough to decide for yourself. I can't make you go then. But I want you to enjoy going to church now so you will want to go when you are older."

"I like church okay," said Rick.

"I'm glad that you feel that way," said Mom. "It makes me happy when our family sits in church together. I never got to do that with my parents when I was little."

Some Questions

1. What do you like about going to church?

2. If you planned a church service, what would you do?

Prayer: Dear God, thank You for the pastor, teachers, musicians, and all the other people at church. Help me enjoy worshiping You. In Jesus' name. Amen.

 ## Devotion 50

The Spirit gives one person a message full of wisdom, while to another person the same Spirit gives a message full of knowledge.
1 Corinthians 12:8

I'm Smart

"The teacher said I was the best reader in my class," Nathan told his mother as he helped set the table for dinner.

"I'm proud of you," said Mom. "I know you like to read."

"That means I'm smart," said Nathan.

"Yes, you are," said his mother, "and being able to read well will help you learn lots of other important things."

"Ben is dumb," said Nathan.

"Why do you say that about your friend?" asked his mother. Ben lived two doors away, and the two boys often played together.

"Because he can't read very well," said Nathan. "He has to point to the words, and he moves his lips when he reads."

"But that doesn't mean he's dumb," said Mom. "When I agreed that you are smart, we were talking about reading. You may not be smart about everything, and Ben is not dumb about everything."

"All the kids laugh when he reads," said Nathan.

"I hope you don't laugh at him," said Mom. "Do you remember when you got your new video game system? You couldn't hook it up, so Ben helped you."

"But he couldn't read the instructions," said Nathan. "I had to do that."

"Yes, but you needed Ben to know how to put all those wires in the right places," said his mother. "He needed you to read, and you needed him to put things together. So each one of you is good in some things, and each one of you needs the other to help with other things."

"Just like us, right Mom?"

"What do you mean?" Mom asked.

"You need me to set the table," said Nathan, "and I need you to cook the dinner."

Some Questions

1. What talents can you use to help others?
2. How do you need others to help you?

> **Prayer:** Holy Spirit, thank You for helping me to know many things. Help me to use my talents to help others, and send others to help me when I can't do something. In Jesus' name. Amen.

 ## Devotion 51

> *Is there anyone among you who is wise and understanding? He is to prove it by his good life, by his good deeds performed with humility and wisdom. James 3:13*

There Was No Reason

Jessica was in her room playing. She heard her father talking on the phone. He put down the phone, came to her room, and knocked on the door.

"Come on, Jessica," Dad said. "You and I are going for a walk."

"I don't want to," she answered. "I'm busy."

"I didn't ask you if you wanted to go for a walk," said

Dad. "You are going with me. I'm busy too, but this is more important."

"Where are we going?" asked Jessica. She could tell by the tone in her father's voice that she had better do what he said.

"You just come with me," said Dad. They went out the back door, down the driveway, and across the street to Mrs. Bower's house. Instead of knocking on the door, Jessica's father led her to the side of the house where Mrs. Bowers had a flower garden. There he pointed at her tulip bed. About 10 tulip stems stood up tall in the little garden. The bright red petals were scattered on the ground.

"Do you know anything about this?" Jessica's father asked.

Jessica looked at the tattered flowers. She remembered how pretty they had been. She also knew she had picked all the petals off the stems. She felt sad as she looked at the naked stems.

"I'm waiting for you to say something," said her father.

"I'm sorry," she said.

"Sorry for what?" asked her father.

"I'm sorry that I ruined the flowers," she said.

"Why did you do it?" her father asked.

Jessica thought. There was no reason. She liked flowers. She liked Mrs. Bowers. She knew she had done it, but she didn't know why.

"I don't know," she answered.

"I understand that," her father answered as he knelt down beside her. "I don't think that you planned to come over here and destroy Mrs. Bowers' flowers. But you did a careless, destructive thing. You took away something that was beautiful, that many people could have enjoyed. Now what should you do?"

"I'll tell Mrs. Bowers I'm sorry," said Jessica.

"And?"

"I'll pay her for the flowers," she added.

"You can't pay for the flowers," her father said. "They are ruined for this year, but they will grow back next year. I talked to Mrs. Bowers, and she said you could pull weeds and grass from her vegetable garden. You go tell her you are ready to pull weeds."

"But I was going to Grandma's house," Jessica said.

"You *were* going," said her father. "But now you are going to Mrs. Bowers' vegetable garden." He dropped on one knee and hugged Jessica. "I love you and forgive you—Jesus does too. But when we hurt something with our sin, we need to take the consequences."

Some Questions

1. Have you seen nice things destroyed because someone was destructive?

2. Why do you think some people destroy things "for no reason"?

Prayer: Thank You, God, for making a beautiful world and for making me clean from sin in Jesus. Help me and others take good care of Your creation. In Jesus' name. Amen.

Devotion 52

[Jesus said,] "I assure you that whoever declares publicly that he belongs to Me, the Son of Man will do the same for him before the angels of God. But whoever rejects Me publicly, the Son of Man will also reject him before the angels of God." Luke 12:8–9

He's My Friend

Jeremy was in his bunk, and the lights were out, but he couldn't go to sleep. This was his first night away from home without his parents. He was at camp. There were five other boys his age in the cabin with him. John, their counselor, an old guy of about 16, had gone to a staff meeting. He had told them all to stay in bed.

At home, Jeremy always said his prayers out loud. Tonight he decided he would just talk to God in his thoughts.

"Let's sneak over and raid the girls' cabin," one voice said.

"We'd better not get out of bed," said another voice. "John told us to stay here."

"You're a wimp," said the first voice. "We're supposed to have fun at camp."

"Ah, Jesus, all of you shut up," said another voice.

"My name's not Jesus," said the first voice. "He's a real wimp."

"Who is?"

"Jesus is."

"Who are you talking about?" asked someone.

"That Jesus guy that they talk about in church," said the first voice. "He's a wimp. He let people beat on Him, and He talked about love stuff. I think that's dumb."

"He's my friend!" said a voice. Jeremy was surprised to realize that he had said it.

"Who said that?"

"I did," said Jeremy. "My name is Jeremy Ross. Jesus let people beat Him up because He loves us. He didn't have to act like a tough guy 'cause He wasn't afraid to die. He wanted to die for us."

"What are you," asked the first voice, "some kind of Sunday school teacher?"

"I just don't want you saying bad things about my Friend," said Jeremy. "So stuff a sock in your mouth and go to sleep."

Some Questions

1. Do you know people who don't know Jesus? Who?

2. How could you tell them about Jesus?

Prayer: Thank You, Jesus, for being my Friend. Would You help my friends also be Your friends? Amen.

Devotion 53

*Again Jesus asked, "What shall I compare
the Kingdom of God with? It is like this. A
woman takes some yeast and mixes it with a
bushel of flour until the whole batch of dough
rises." Luke 13:20–21*

You Can Change Tomorrow

Tiffany and her family were eating dinner Friday
evening. Her parents were talking about the projects they
planned to do the next day.

"I don't like Saturdays," said Tiffany.

"Why not?" asked her mother.

" 'Cause it's always the same old thing," said Tiffany.
"I have to clean my room and do homework."

"If I remember right," said her father, "you spend most
of the morning watching TV."

"That's what I mean," she said. "It's always the same
old thing. Mom will go shopping. Dad will work at the
computer."

"We could change tomorrow," said her mother.

"No, we can't," said Tiffany. "Today is Friday.
Tomorrow has to be Saturday. That's the way it is."

"But we could change what we *do* on Saturday," said
her mother.

"But you always say those things have to be done,"
said Tiffany.

"Okay, I do have some shopping, and you do have to
clean your room," said her mother.

"And I do have to work on some income tax records," said her father. "But I could work on the computer tonight instead of watching the ball game."

"You could clean your room tonight," said her mother. "Then you could do your homework early in the morning while you are fresh, instead of watching cartoons on TV. I could read the grocery ads and sort my coupons tonight so I could get my shopping done early tomorrow."

"Then we'd all be done with the things we have to do before lunch," said her father. "What could we do in the afternoon?"

"We could go to a movie," said her mother.

"Or play miniature golf," said Tiffany.

"Or take a picnic out to the park and go fishing," said Dad.

"I'm looking forward to tomorrow," said Tiffany.

"Sounds to me as though we can look forward to lots of Saturdays," said her father.

Some Questions

1. What can you do to change things when you are bored?

2. How can you help your family plan some fun things?

Prayer: Dear God, thank You for the gift of time. Help me do the things that I have to do first so I have time to do the things I want to do. In Jesus' name. Amen.

Devotion 54

Put yourselves to the test and judge your-
selves, to find out whether you are living in
faith. Surely you know that Christ Jesus is
in you?—unless you have completely failed.
2 Corinthians 13:5

What Do You Think You Should Do?

Chuck sat on his bed. He could not believe what had happened to him in the last hour. Only 60 minutes ago he was walking home from school. Everything was fine. He didn't have a trouble in the world.

His friend Ryan said he had to go into a store to buy some batteries for his radio. Chuck had gone along. While Ryan bought the batteries, Chuck looked at the CD rack. He had no money with him and didn't need any more CDs anyway. Then he saw one that he wanted. Without even thinking, he put it in his pocket. He and Ryan walked out of the store.

Then Chuck's whole world fell apart. A security officer stopped him and asked to see his sales slip. From then on everything was a blur. Ryan kept saying, "Why did you do such a stupid thing? I had some money. I would have loaned it to you."

The officer made Chuck call his parents and tell them what he had done. Then the security man took the phone and talked. Chuck couldn't hear what his dad was saying. Then his dad came and got him. They said nothing during the drive home.

"Son, I need some time to think about this," said his dad when they got home. "I'm too angry and hurt to talk about it now. You need to think about what has happened too. Go to your room; I'll be in later."

So Chuck sat in his room. He tried to think about what had happened, but he didn't like to see and hear those things again. He tried to forget what had happened, but it kept coming back. He could see the surprised look on Ryan's face. He could feel his father's anger. He wondered what his father would do to him. Would he go to jail? Would his parents send him to a place for bad kids? What would happen to him at school? Chuck was both relieved and worried when his father came into his room.

"I called your mother at work," said Dad. "We talked about what has happened."

"What are you going to do to me?" Chuck asked.

"We talked about that," his dad answered. "You made a mistake, a serious mistake. But we understand that you know better. We don't have to tell you that what you did is wrong."

"I'm sorry, Dad," Chuck said.

"I know you are," said Dad. "Your mother and I have always trusted you. We talked about it, and we discovered that we still trust you. So we are going to ask you to be responsible for what you did."

"What do you mean?" asked Chuck.

"Instead of deciding how to punish you," his dad said, "we are going to ask you to tell us what should be done. We know you forgot some of the things we have taught you when you took the CD. Now we want to see if you remember."

"What things?" Chuck asked.

"Let's think about it," said Dad. "What should you have thought about when you were in the store?"

"I should have remembered that stealing is wrong," said Chuck.

"Yes, you know that," said Dad. "Have we also taught you what you should do when you do something wrong?"

"Yes," said Chuck. "I should ask Jesus to forgive me. And I should ask the man at the store to forgive me."

"I'm glad that you remember that," said Dad. "If you had remembered that in the store, would it have helped you?"

"If I had thought about Jesus," said Chuck, "I don't think I would have taken the CD."

"And now?" asked Dad.

"Well, I put the CD back," said Chuck. "But I'll go down to the store and talk to the man. I'll say I'm sorry and ask if I can work at the store or do something to help him know I'm sorry."

"That sounds like a good idea," said Dad. "You need to learn to live out your faith yourself. Your mother and I can't make you be good, but we can love you. And Jesus loves you—enough to have died for you so you can be forgiven."

"Thanks, Dad," said Chuck. "Will you go to the store with me?"

Some Questions

1. Jesus forgives you when you sin. How does He help you avoid sin?

2. What would you do if you did something like Chuck did?

3. How can your parents help you when you have a problem?

Prayer: Dear Jesus, be with me when I am tempted to do something wrong and help me do what is right. Amen.

 ## Devotion 55

I pray that your love will keep on growing more and more, together with true knowledge and perfect judgment, so that you will be able to choose what is best.
Philippians 1:9–10a

You Don't Vote on This

Jamie waited until the news was over and her father had turned off the TV.

"Daddy," she said, "can I talk to you about something important?"

"Of course, you can, sweetie," her dad said. "For this conversation should you sit on my lap or sit beside me?"

"I'll sit here," Jamie said as she chose a chair facing her father. She thought a minute and then said, "I want to move back to where we used to live."

"Why?" her dad asked.

"Because all my friends live there," she said, "and the school was better. And we lived closer to Grandma and Grandpa."

"Those things are important to your mother and me too," Dad said. "Do you remember why we moved?"

" 'Cause the place where you worked closed down and you didn't have a job," said Jamie.

"That's right," said Dad. "We had to move for the good of our whole family."

"But maybe you could get a job back there now," Jamie said. "I got a letter from my friend Kara, and her daddy got a new job."

"I'm glad he did," Dad answered. "But I may not find a job by our old home, and we're all settled here. Before long you'll make friends and enjoy being here too."

"But I don't want to live here," Jamie said. "I vote that we move back."

"Honey, your vote can't change the decision," Dad said. "Your mother and I had to decide what was best for our whole family."

"But that's not fair," Jamie said. "I'm a part of this family too."

"You're an important part of the family," said Dad. "We let you help make some decisions."

"When?" she asked.

"We let you help pick out the color for your room," said Dad. "When we go to a movie or out to dinner we all talk it over, and you get a vote too."

"Okay," Jamie said. "You can decide where we eat and what movie we see. I'll decide where we will live."

Her dad smiled. "First you have to learn how to make decisions about little things. Then you'll be able to make good decisions when you're old enough to take care of yourself."

"I can make pretty good decisions now," Jamie said.

"I agree," her dad said. "How about deciding that you will make friends here and learn to enjoy our new home?"

Some Questions

1. What kind of decisions can you make for yourself now?

2. When do you need help as you make a decision?

3. What decisions do parents and others have to make for you?

Prayer: Dear God, help me make good choices and help me understand the decisions that others have to make for me. In Jesus' name. Amen.

 ## Devotion 56

He [The LORD] lets me rest in fields of green grass and leads me to quiet pools of fresh water. He gives me new strength. He guides me in the right paths, as He has promised.
Psalm 23:2–3

What Are You Doing? Nothing

"What are you doing, Julian?" Mr. Sharbol asked his grandson as he joined him on the back porch.

"Nothing," Julian answered.

"That's amazing!" his grandfather answered. "I didn't

think it was possible to do nothing. Would you teach me how?"

"You already know how to do nothing," laughed Julian. "I've seen you do nothing lots of times."

"When?"

"Well, sometimes you come out here in the backyard and just sit," said Julian. "You don't have any music to listen to or a newspaper to read or anything."

"But I'm doing a lot when I come out here," protested Grandfather.

"What?"

"I dream about the past and plan the future," his grandfather said. "I think about what I did when I was your age, and I think about what you will be doing when you are as old as I am now."

"That doesn't sound like doing anything to me," Julian said. "I like to do exciting things."

"Like what?" Grandfather asked.

"I like to play soccer and go roller-blading," Julian said. "I like to listen to music and play video games."

"Those sound like fun things," said his grandfather. "I never got to do those things when I was a kid, though we did play softball. And I went fishing and hunting a lot. But I learned some important things that I still like to do. Come with me and I'll show you."

Mr. Sharbol led his grandson to the back of the garage to a quiet part of the backyard. He lay down in the grass under a big tree and motioned for Julian to do the same. The two of them were silent for a while.

"This is boring," said Julian. "We're not doing anything."

"I'm doing something," said Grandfather.

"What are you doing?"

"I'm listening to things," he said. "What do you hear?"

Julian listened for a while. "I hear cars on the street," he said, "and I hear Mom and Grandma talking in the house. I hear someone playing music and a television somewhere."

Grandfather said nothing. "And I hear some birds in the tree," added Julian, "and the bees buzzing in the flowers. And I hear Toby panting 'cause he's hot. I hear you breathing and my heart beating."

"What do you see?" Grandfather asked.

"I see the birds in the tree above us," said Julian, "and I see little apples on the tree that will grow big this summer. I see two airplanes in the sky and lots of clouds."

"What do the clouds look like?" Grandfather asked.

"That one looks like the water slide at the park," said Julian, pointing, "and that one looks like a pterodactyl, and there's a Tyrannosaurus rex."

"What do you smell?" asked Grandfather.

"I smell the roses by the fence and the dirt by the tree," Julian answered. "I smell coffee. That means Grandma has something for us to eat. I'll beat you to the house."

Grandfather tried to race, but by the time he was up, Julian was already on the steps of the porch and headed into the house.

"Where have you two men been?" Julian's grandmother asked.

"Out behind the garage," Julian answered.

"What were you doing?"

"Nothing."

Some Questions

1. Do you have time to be by yourself to think and dream and pray?

2. Do you sometimes get so busy that you feel upset and worried? What can you do about those times?

3. Are you sometimes bored and don't have enough to do? What can you do then?

Prayer: Holy Spirit, help me see and hear all the beautiful things in the world and give me time to enjoy them. In Jesus' name. Amen.

Devotion 57

The attitude you should have is the one that Christ Jesus had. Philippians 2:5

He Has an Attitude

The Rolling family was happy. They had moved to a new house and discovered new friends living next door. The parents were about the same age and liked to do the same things. Each family had a 9-year-old boy, Carl Rolling and Bruce Jacobs.

The Jacobs family invited the new neighbors over for dinner on the first Saturday that they lived next door to one another. They had a lot of fun at the dinner. Mr. Jacobs played a new video game with Carl while Carl's dad told Bruce about the wildlife museum where they used to live.

Later the boys went outside to play.

"Your dad sure is nice," said Carl.

"That's what you think," answered Bruce.

"I thought he was nice to me," answered Carl.

"He just watches TV, and he yells if I make any noise," said Bruce. "He hardly ever talks to me except when we have company."

Meanwhile in the house the two sets of parents were getting better acquainted.

"We are so glad that Carl has a boy his age living next door," said Mrs. Rolling, "and Bruce seems like such a fine young boy."

"I'm glad you think so," said Mr. Jacobs, "and I hope that a new friend like Carl will help him."

"What do you mean?" asked Mr. Rolling.

"Bruce has an attitude and is hard to live with," said Mr. Jacobs.

"But he seemed like such a pleasant boy at dinner," said Mrs. Rolling. "We enjoyed being with him."

"Sure," said Mr. Jacobs, "that's because we have company. Usually he pouts or complains about something. I hope that he will learn good habits from Carl."

Some Questions

1. Does your family act differently in some ways when you have company?

2. What attitudes in other members of your family do you think should be changed?

3. Which of your attitudes do other members of your family think you should change?

Prayer: Holy Spirit, help us use our best behavior and our best attitudes with our own family. Forgive us when we have the wrong kind of attitude. Amen.

Devotion 58

"Do not be worried and upset," Jesus told them. "Believe in God and believe also in Me." John 14:1

Are You Worried?

Megan walked into her sister's room. Usually Casey yelled at her if she came in without asking. But she knew Casey wouldn't yell tonight.

"Are you worried?" Megan asked.

"You mean because Mom and Dad are mad at each other?" Casey responded.

"Yeah," Megan said. "Do you think they'll get a divorce?"

"I don't know," said Casey. "Beth's parents always got into arguments like that, and they got divorced."

"In Sunday school the teacher said Jesus told us not to be worried and upset," said Megan. "Are we bad if we are worried and upset? 'Cause I am."

"I think Jesus said that because He knows we *do* get worried and upset," said Casey.

"But He does tell us not to do it," said Megan.

"That's because He promises to help us and be with us

when we have a problem," said Casey. "I guess we should pray for Mom and Dad."

"I told Grandma that Mom and Dad had arguments," said Megan. "She said that people disagree sometimes. She said Mom and Dad can argue and have problems and still love each other and not get a divorce."

"I heard them talking together a long time after they quit arguing," said Casey. "But I couldn't hear what they were saying."

"Maybe that's good," said Megan. "We can hear them when they are mad at each other because they yell. When they like each other, they don't have to yell."

"Let's wait until bedtime," said Casey, "then you ask Mom and I'll ask Dad if they got over their argument. Okay?"

Some Questions

1. Do you worry about some things you have heard your parents say?

2. How could you talk to them about it so you don't have to worry anymore?

3. How will Jesus help you when you are worried and upset?

Prayer: Dear God, I don't understand a lot of things that happen. Will You help me figure out a way to find out what is going on? In Jesus' name. Amen.

Devotion 59

If you become angry, do not let your anger lead you into sin, and do not stay angry all day. Ephesians 4:26

No One Can Make You Angry

Chuck's father picked him and his friend Peter up at soccer practice. As they drove toward Peter's house, Chuck's dad had to stop because a delivery truck was double-parked on the street. Cars were coming from the other way, so they had to sit and wait.

"Why don't you blow your horn?" Chuck asked his dad.

"My dad says those kind of drivers make him mad," said Peter. "He yells at them and says things that he won't let me say."

"Doesn't that driver make you angry, Dad?" Chuck asked.

"No," said his father. "I used to get angry when people did things like that. But I don't anymore."

"Why not?" Peter asked. "My dad would get angry."

"We had a discussion about anger in our Bible class, and I learned something important."

"What?" Peter asked.

"I learned that when I was angry, it was not because other people made me angry but because I let myself get angry," said Chuck's dad.

"But how do you keep from getting angry when people do dumb things?" asked Chuck.

"First, I remember that the driver is in a hurry too," said his dad. "Then I remember I have done some dumb things too. Jesus forgives me, so I guess I can afford to forgive others without getting ticked off about it."

"But you get angry at me sometimes, Dad," said Chuck.

"Hey, I didn't say I was perfect," his father laughed.

"Look," said Peter. "Here comes the driver now."

Some Questions

1. When do you get angry?

2. When you are angry, should you pretend that you are not? What should you do?

3. How will Jesus help you handle your anger?

Prayer: Dear Jesus, I am glad that You can love me and not be angry at me, even when I do wrong things. Please don't let my anger make me hurt other people. Amen.

 ## Devotion 60

For since we have become one with Him in dying as He did, in the same way we shall be one with Him by being raised to life as He was. Romans 6:5

Did Jesus Die for Grandpa?

Cindy sat in the backseat of the car as her family drove

home from church on Good Friday. She had tears in her eyes.

"Did you hear what he said?" she asked.

"What who said?" her mother asked.

"Pastor," she answered. "He said Jesus died for us so we wouldn't have to die."

"That's right," her mother replied. "Good Friday is a special day for us because we remember that God loved us so much that He let Jesus die in our place."

"Didn't God love Grandpa?" Cindy asked. Her grandfather had died three weeks earlier.

"Oh, yes," said her mother. "God loves Grandpa just as He loves us."

"I thought about your grandfather during church too," said Dad. "I'm glad that he believed in Jesus."

"But if Jesus died for Grandpa, why did Grandpa have to die?" Cindy asked.

"I see what you mean," said Mom. "When we talk about death, we have two meanings. When we say Jesus died for us, we mean that He died on the cross to pay the price for our sins. Remember when Jesus said, 'My God, My God, why have You abandoned Me?' That's what we mean when we say Jesus died for us. We don't ever have to be without God, even after we die, because Jesus rose from the dead and so will we."

"But Grandpa still died," Cindy said.

"Yes, and so will we," said Mom. "When Grandpa died in the hospital, that was the other meaning of death. He died and left us to go be with God in heaven. We don't have to be afraid of that kind of death because it doesn't last. And it doesn't last because Jesus took the other kind of death away for us."

"Then God loves us, even when we die?" Cindy asked.

"Yes," said her mother. "Remember when we went to Grandpa's funeral? We could talk about his death because we know he lives with Jesus now."

"I'm glad we went to church tonight," said Cindy.

Some Questions

1. Do you have any questions you want to ask about dying?

2. If one of your friends is worried about death, what could you tell him or her?

Prayer: Dear Jesus, thank You for loving us and for dying for us so we can live with You now and forever. Amen.

 ## Devotion 61

Some people spend their money freely and still grow richer. Others are cautious, and yet grow poorer. Proverbs 11:24

The Story of Three $5 Bills

"Look how much money I have," said Shanna as she came out of her room. "$15."

"How did you get that much money?" asked her father.

"I found this one on the sidewalk when I was coming home from school," Shanna said. "It was just lying there, so I had no way to find out who owned it." She added that because she knew her dad would ask. "Aunt Joan gave me this one for my birthday, and you paid me this one because I helped you clean the garage last Saturday. Remember, I worked a long time to get it."

"You do have a lot of money," said Dad, "but do you know that those $5 bills are not worth the same amount?"

"Yes, they are," she answered. "Each is worth $5."

"But they still have different values," said her Dad, "because of the way you received each one."

"What do you mean?" Shanna asked.

"Look at the one I paid you for work that you did," said Dad. "That is worth $5, but I think it's worth even more because it shows that you can earn money. You were a good worker last Saturday, and you deserved your pay."

"That means I could earn even more," said Shanna.

"Right," said Dad. "Now look at the one Aunt Joan gave you. What makes it have a special value?"

" 'Cause Aunt Joan thought about me and remembered my birthday," said Shanna.

"Right again," said Dad. "That money has a special value because it shows someone loves you. Now look at the last one."

"I found it," she said.

"Yes," said Dad. "It is worth $5 when you spend it, but it doesn't have any lasting value. You won't find money on a sidewalk very often. It doesn't give anything to you except what you buy with it."

"You're trying to teach me how to manage my money, aren't you?" asked Shanna.

"Yes," said Dad, "because money has different values according to how we get it and how we spend it. Before I spend my paycheck, I put some money aside for church. If you spend money wisely, you will gain from having had the money. You could just waste the money and get nothing for it. Or you could even use it to buy something that would hurt you."

"Are you going to tell me how to spend it?" Shanna asked.

"No, it's your money," Dad said. "You know how hard you worked to earn one of those $5 bills. I think you'll spend it wisely."

"You're right, Dad," Shanna said. "And I'll save some for church too."

Some Questions

1. What have you done with money that made you happy?

2. What have you done with money that was a mistake?

Prayer: Father in heaven, thank You for blessing me with money. Bless me with good sense so I can make good use of the money. In Jesus' name. Amen.

 Devotion 62

"Do not be worried and upset," Jesus told them. "Believe in God and believe also in Me." John 14:1

I Don't Want to Talk about It

Brenda was scared. She was sitting in Pastor Allen's office. She had been going to church since she had lived with her grandparents, so she knew the pastor. But she had not talked to him alone before.

"I'm glad you get to come to church with your grandparents, Brenda," Pastor Allen said. "Since you are going to be living with them for a while, I'd like to get acquainted with you."

"I'm in the fourth grade," said Brenda. She knew adults always asked about school.

"I hope you like your new school," Pastor said. "Your grandmother told me that your parents are divorced. She also told me about some of the things you have heard and seen when your mother and father had problems."

"I don't want to talk about it," said Brenda.

"I understand that," said Pastor Allen. "Let me tell you something about me. I spend a lot of time with people who have problems like divorces. I see how they are angry and sad and lonely. I see how people who love them are hurt too. I understand why you don't want to talk about your family. Could I tell you about other families that have divorces?"

"Okay," Brenda said.

"Sometimes people who get a divorce become very angry," said Pastor Allen. "They say bad things, and some even hit each other. If their children hear and see those things, it scares them. Sometimes the children think it is their fault. But the boys and girls have not done anything wrong. I tell them that Jesus loves them and is with them. He will help take away the hurt and the fear, and He will love and forgive the moms and dads who hurt each other."

Brenda sat very still. She was listening, but she still didn't say anything.

"Sometimes I talk to big people, as old as your parents, who still are sad because of things that happened when they were children. They are still angry at their parents. They are still afraid to love anyone," continued Pastor Allen. "I don't want that to happen to you. I know you are sad and afraid now, but Jesus will help you so you can be happy again. You can live with your grandparents and see a happy family. You can come to church and be with people who know Jesus helps them when they are sad and hurt."

"But do you think I can ever live with my mom and dad?" Brenda asked.

"Your parents still love you, even though they have so many problems that they can't show that love right now," said Pastor Allen. "I think God gave you me and your grandparents to love you until your mom and dad get help for their problems. I want you to know that you have friends, and I want to be one of those friends."

"Can I come back and see you again?" Brenda asked.

"Yes," Pastor Allen said. "We'll make an appointment right now."

Some Questions

1. Are their things you don't want to talk about but you would like to know about?

2. Who can you talk to when you are worried or feel bad?

Prayer: Dear Jesus, be with all families that have problems and help them. Bless our family and help us talk to each other and forgive each other. Amen.

Devotion 63

Offer yourselves as a living sacrifice to God, dedicated to His service and pleasing to Him. This is the true worship that you should offer.
Romans 12:1b

Do I Have to Play Basketball?

Greg and his family had moved to a new city. That meant they had to get used to a new home, new school, new church, and new friends. After the first week of school, Greg had a problem. He decided to ask his dad for help.

"Dad," Greg said, "you liked to play basketball when you were in school, right?"

"Yes," Dad answered. "I played basketball for a long time, and I still like to watch it."

"I'm the tallest kid in my new class," Greg said. "When the coach saw me, he asked me to try out for the basketball team. I don't want to."

"You don't have to play basketball just because I did," said Dad.

"The coach doesn't know you, so that's no problem," Greg answered. "He said that God made me tall, so I have to use that gift to play basketball. Is that true?"

"Well, it's partly true," said Dad. "You have a strong, healthy body, and that is a gift from God. God wants you to take care of your body, and sports help you stay in shape, but you can decide on the best sports for you."

"I like to play soccer," said Greg, "and I think I'll go out for the track team."

"Sounds good to me," said Dad. "You tell your coach that. I bet he'll understand."

Some Questions

1. What do you do to get exercise and stay in good physical condition?

2. How do you take care of your body?

Prayer: Dear God, thank You for good health and strong bodies. Bless those who are sick or who have physical problems. In Jesus' name. Amen.

 ## Devotion 64

Each one should give, then, as he has decided, not with regret or out of a sense of duty; for God loves the one who gives gladly.
2 Corinthians 9:7

A Family Meeting

"Dad and Mom said they want all of us to come to the kitchen," Becky called to her two brothers one morning.

"We already had breakfast," said Aaron, "and it's too early for lunch."

"I bet Dad has found a new game he wants us to learn," said Sammy.

"Sounds more like they want to talk about homework or household chores," said Becky.

The family gathered around the kitchen table. The adults had a cup of coffee, and each child had a cup of cocoa and some cookies.

"It's time for a family meeting," said their dad. "We have something we want to show you." He put a box on the kitchen table. The children were curious.

"Yesterday was payday for both of us," their mother said. "We decided that you are old enough to learn about paychecks and bills." She passed the two paychecks around to the children.

"Wow!" said Sammy, "You make a lot of money!"

"We're rich!" said Becky.

"That's what we thought you would think," said Dad. "But you'd better wait to see what else is in this box."

"First, here are our church offering envelopes," said Mom. "Our family gives a tithe—that's 10 percent—of our income to church. We write that check first." Dad was writing a check to put in the envelope.

"You give away that much money?" asked Aaron.

"Yes," said Dad. "We are happy that Jesus is a part of our lives. This is one way to thank Him and help ourselves and others learn more about Him."

"The next check is the payment on our house mortgage," said their mother as she picked up the checkbook. "Some families pay rent. We have to write a check like this every month for about 17 more years, then we'll have the house paid for."

"Then we have utility bills," said Dad as he pulled a stack of envelopes from the box. "We pay for our electricity, gas, water, and telephone. That's why we ask you to turn off the lights when you leave a room and not to waste water."

The three children looked at the bills as the parents wrote more checks.

"Then we have a credit card payment," said Dad. "We only *have* to pay $35 this month, but we will pay it all so we won't have to pay interest."

"What's *interest*?" Aaron asked.

"That's money the bank charges for letting us use its money," Mom said. "The bank also pays us interest if we let it use our money."

"The bank pays interest on my savings account," said Becky.

"That's right," said Mom. "Some months we also have insurance and tax bills, so we try to put a little in our savings account so we can pay the big bills when they are due."

"Are we done now?" asked Sammy.

"No," said Dad. "Since we're careful about saving money, we'll have enough for a treat tonight. How about pizza?"

"It's a deal," said Mom.

Some Questions

1. What do you know about your family's income and expenses?

2. How can you help your family make good use of money?

Prayer: Dear God, thank You for the money we have in our family. Help us to use it wisely and to give our first gifts to You. In Jesus' name. Amen.

Devotion 65

But the truth is that Christ has been raised from death, as the guarantee that those who sleep in death will also be raised.
1 Corinthians 15:20

I'll Make Them Spell Your Name Right

The Rajczyk family lived in a new house on the edge of town. When they drove to and from their home, they always went by an old cemetery with many big tombstones. Mark liked to talk about the cemetery. Several times he had talked his parents into stopping at the big iron gate so they could walk down the long paths.

"Don't worry," Mark told his parents one day after they had driven by the cemetery. "When you die, I'll make them spell your name right."

"What are you talking about?" his dad asked.

"I mean in the cemetery," Mark said. "I'll make them spell *Rajczyk* right on your tombstone."

"We appreciate that," said Dad. He and Mom laughed because they were used to the fact that very few people could spell their name correctly. They realized that Mark also had to spell it over and over again for other people.

"Why do you want to be sure our name is spelled correctly on our tombstones?" asked Mom.

"Because Jesus is going to come to make you alive again," said Mark, "and I want Him to be able to find you."

"You're paying more attention to what happens in church than I thought," said Dad. "Do you remember the first thing we did on Easter?"

"Sure," Mark said. "Pastor said, 'He is risen,' and we said, 'He is risen indeed!' I liked that part."

"And you know what those words mean for us?" asked Mom.

"Sure," Mark said. "Jesus broke out of His grave, and He'll get us out of ours too."

"Even if our name is misspelled on the tombstone?" asked his Dad.

"I guess so," Mark said. "But I'll make sure it's right."

Some Questions

1. Has anyone in your family died? Do you know where he or she is buried?

2. Why do we know we will be raised from the dead?

Prayer: Thank You, Jesus, for living a perfect life for us, for dying for us, and for being alive again so You can be with us now. Amen.

Devotion 66

Keep on imitating me, my brothers. Pay attention to those who follow the right example that we have set for you. Philippians 3:17

What Grade Are You In?

Kyle was on vacation with his parents. They had driven a long way to see his grandparents and lots of other relatives that Kyle had never met before. One day he stayed with his Aunt Martha while his parents visited someone in a nursing home.

"Aren't you going to ask me what grade I'm in?" asked Kyle.

"Should I?" asked Aunt Martha.

"All adults ask kids what grade they're in," said Kyle.

"I already know you just finished the fourth grade," said Aunt Martha. "Are you going to ask me what grade I'm in?"

"You're too old to be in school anymore," said Kyle.

"But I'm not too old to learn something," said Aunt Martha, "so I can still be in some grade."

"Okay," said Kyle, who was beginning to like Aunt Martha. "What grade are you in?"

"I'm in grade 27," said Aunt Martha.

"Grades don't go that high," said Kyle. "They only go to 12 or 14 or something like that."

"But I'm in grade 27," said Aunt Martha.

"What school are you in?" Kyle asked.

"The school of life," said Aunt Martha.

"That's not a real school."

"Oh yes, it is," said Aunt Martha. "I bet I'm learning as much in grade 27 as you did in grade four."

"How do you figure you are in grade 27?" asked Kyle.

"Because when I was 6 years old, I was in grade one, said Aunt Martha. "I have never failed a grade, and I have learned something each year. I am now 33 years old so that makes me in grade 27."

"What grade is my daddy in?" Kyle asked.

"Let's see," said Aunt Martha. "He's two years older than I am, so he is in grade 29."

"And Grandpa?" asked Kyle.

"Let's see, he was 30 when I was born so that makes him in grade 57," said Aunt Martha.

"Are you sure other people know about these grades?" asked Kyle.

"No, but you and I do," said Aunt Martha. "Isn't that enough?"

Some Questions

1. What are the most important things that you have learned this year?

2. Does everything you learn come from school?

3. How will you keep on learning after you are out of school?

Prayer: Holy Spirit, You are a good teacher. Help me to be a good student in school and in the rest of life too. In Jesus' name. Amen.

Devotion 67

Parents, do not treat your children in such a way as to make them angry. Instead, raise them with Christian discipline and instruction.
Ephesians 6:4

I Don't Like That

Kyle enjoyed being on vacation with all of his mother's family—even if there weren't many children around. One evening when all the adults were talking after dinner, Kyle fell asleep. His father carried him upstairs to bed.

"That's a great kid you have there, Janet," her brother, Paul, said to Kyle's mother. "Somehow it's still difficult for me to think of you as a mother."

"Maybe that's because you aren't married and won't have kids of your own for a while," replied Janet. "I noticed you and Kyle were out in the yard together today. How did you do as an uncle?"

"I'm not sure," answered Paul. "Kids are different today than they were when I grew up."

"Still having trouble tying your shoes?" teased Janet.

"Don't tell Kyle that story," said Paul. "No, but when we went out in the yard, I tousled his hair—just as my uncles all used to do to me. And you know what he said? He said, 'Please don't. I don't like that.' "

"Do you think that was rude?" Janet asked.

"No, but I wouldn't have talked to an adult that way when I was a kid," said Paul.

"Did you like it when adults messed up your hair at that age?" his sister asked.

"No, I hated it," answered Paul.

"Then why did you do it to Kyle?" she asked.

" 'Cause that's what uncles do, I guess," said Paul.

"I'm glad Kyle told you what he did," said Janet. "I think it was better for him to tell you than to be unhappy with you."

"Did he learn to do that from you?" asked Paul.

"I guess so," answered Janet. "Mike and I want Kyle to be honest with people. We don't think children should be put down by adults. And we've told him to speak up if something makes him uncomfortable."

"I didn't mean to make him uncomfortable."

"I know you didn't," his sister answered. "You'll learn if you ever have children. It's important for them to be polite, but they need to learn to do it in an honest way."

Some Questions

1. Do you see yourself as a polite person?

2. Do you think of yourself as an honest person?

3. What will you say and do if you find yourself in an uncomfortable situation?

Prayer: Dear God, help me to be kind to others—and also kind to myself. In Jesus' name. Amen.

Devotion 68

Your lives will be filled with the truly good
qualities which only Jesus Christ can pro-
duce, for the glory and praise of God.
Philippians 1:11

What Will You Be Responsible For?

After his parents divorced, Mike knew he would spend
every other week with his father. The first week did not
go well. Mike and his dad spent a lot of time together.
They ate most of their meals in a restaurant. They went
to a movie on Saturday. But it wasn't fun. Mike didn't
feel at home at his dad's house. His dad treated him as if
he were company rather than part of a family.

"I think we've got to do things differently this week,"
Dad said when Mike came for his next week. "We had
fun the last time, but now we've got to learn to be a family when we are together."

"Okay," said Mike. "You be the dad, and I'll be the
kid."

"That's a good start," said Dad. "Now let's decide what
I am responsible for because I am the dad. I've got a
place for us to live, and you have your own bedroom. I'll
bring home the groceries to feed us."

"You've got to drive the car," said Mike, "and pay the
bills."

"Okay," said Dad. "What are you responsible for?"

"I'll watch TV," said Mike, "and I'll eat without complaining."

"Good start," said Dad. "But it's my job to say which TV programs you watch and how much too. The last time you were here you seemed to think it was my job to get you out of bed in the morning."

"Mom always does," said Mike.

"That's okay at your other home," said Dad. "At this house it is your job to get out of bed. I'll call you one time."

"I'll try," said Mike, "and I'll help set the table and put the dishes in the dishwasher."

"I'll clean my room, and you clean yours," said Dad. "We'll work together on the rest of the house. I'll take out the garbage if you bring in the newspaper."

"Okay," said Mike. He didn't feel as though he were company anymore. He was at home.

Some Questions

1. What are you responsible for at your home?

2. Would you feel better if you had a list of all the things you are supposed to do to help your family?

Prayer: God our Father, thank You for the people who live with me and help them be glad that I live with them. In Jesus' name. Amen.

Devotion 69

[Jesus said,] "If you forgive others the
wrongs they have done to you, your Father
in heaven will also forgive you. But if you
do not forgive others, then your Father will
not forgive the wrongs you have done."
Matthew 6:14–15

Learning How to Forgive

One day Taylor borrowed her twin sister Tiffany's red
sweater without asking. On the way home from school
someone pushed Taylor, and she fell into a puddle. The
red sweater was wet and dirty. When Tiffany saw her
sweater, she was angry with her sister and said she was
going to take anything she wanted from Taylor's side of
the closet.

"I'm sorry," said Taylor. "I know I should have asked
you first, but you were already gone when I wanted to
borrow it."

"But look at my sweater," said Tiffany. "It's ruined. I
wanted to wear it tomorrow."

About that time the twins' mother came into their room
with a plate of fresh cookies. She heard the girls arguing.

"What's going on in here?" asked Mom.

"Taylor took my sweater without asking," said Tiffany.
"Then she got it all wet and dirty."

"I said I was sorry," said Taylor, "but she won't forgive
me."

"No, I won't forgive you," said Tiffany. "You have to

pay for my sweater. I want a new one."

"Okay, both of you, calm down," said Mom. "Tiffany, remember when you broke my bathroom mirror? I forgave you."

"I don't care," said Tiffany. "She should have asked me first."

"I think you both need to learn about forgiveness," said Mom. "Let's pretend this plate of cookies is forgiveness. I'm going to put it here across the room. Now, Tiffany, you don't want Taylor to have any cookies, so you hold her over there."

The two girls watched their mother as she put the cookies across the room. Tiffany was glad to grab hold of Taylor's arm so her sister couldn't go for a cookie.

"Now, Tiffany," said Mom, "as long as you keep Taylor from coming to get a cookie, you can't reach one either."

The two girls looked at the cookies across the room. They were both hungry, but Taylor couldn't go get a cookie because her sister was holding her. Tiffany could not go get a cookie because she didn't want Taylor to have one.

"Now you can understand something that Jesus teaches about forgiveness," said Mom. "He wants us all to be forgiven, and He died to pay for all our sins. But He tells us that we need to share His forgiveness by forgiving one another."

"If I go get a cookie, does that mean I forgive Taylor?" asked Tiffany.

"I think that would be one way to show your forgiveness," said Mom. "Remember Jesus has already forgiven both of you. You might as well enjoy the gift He gave you."

"Okay," said Tiffany. "Let's eat cookies."

Some Questions

1. Are there some people that you do not want to forgive?

2. Does Jesus want to forgive the ones that you don't want to forgive?

3. How can Jesus help you forgive others?

Prayer: Dear Jesus, forgive our sins as we forgive those who sin against us. Amen.

 ## Devotion 70

My dear friend, do not imitate what is bad, but imitate what is good. 3 John 11a

Why Do We Need Manners?

"Are we having company for dinner tonight?" Lauren asked her mother.

"No, just family," said her mother.

"Then why are you setting the dining room table?" asked Lauren.

"Because I want to have a nice meal," said Mom, "and I want all of us to have a chance to practice our good manners."

"Oh, no," said Lauren. "Not one of those meals!"

"Yes, one of those meals," said Mom. "I think all of us

need to know how to come to the table at the same time, to have good conversation, to use good table manners, and to stay until everyone is finished."

"I'd rather eat from a tray while I watch TV," said Lauren.

"We do that sometimes," said Mom, "but you also need to learn how to have good manners."

"Why?" asked Lauren. "It's not fun to eat that way."

"But that's the exact reason we need to learn good manners," said Mom. "Being polite doesn't mean you have to be a fake and not have any fun. We need to learn to eat and talk in a way that is pleasant and comfortable—for us and for company too."

"I'm not comfortable when I have to think about sitting straight and using the right fork and stuff like that," said Lauren.

"But some day you will be very uncomfortable if you don't know how to eat properly in a restaurant or at a special dinner. Politeness is a way to help others and to help yourself."

"I eat with other kids at school," said Lauren, "and some of them don't have *any* manners. Kevin chews with his mouth open, and Gretchen stuffs food into her mouth."

"Do you like to watch them eat?" asked Mom.

"No," said Lauren.

"Proves my point," said Mom. "Remember to put an extra fork at each plate because those who still have a clean fork after we finish the meal will get a piece of chocolate pie."

Some Questions

1. What rules of politeness does your family have for meals?

2. Do members of your family think they need better table manners?

3. What prayer do you say at mealtime?

A Table Prayer: Come, Lord Jesus, eat with our family. Help us enjoy the food and the people who are at the table with us. Amen.

 ## Devotion 71

[Jesus said,] "A healthy tree bears good fruit, but a poor tree bears bad fruit."
Matthew 7:17

What's Wrong with Your Brother?

"Let's go back to my room," Dan said to his new friend, Vince, after dinner. Dan was happy to have a friend who could come to his house. Their family had moved to a new town, and Dan had been lonely for his old friends. But he knew that Vince would become a good friend.

"Wow, you've got lots of caps," said Vince.

"That's not even all of them," said Dan. "We don't have them all unpacked. I've got a cap from every place my dad has traveled."

"What's wrong with your brother?" asked Vince as he

tried on some of Dan's caps.

"Wrong?" Dan asked. "There's nothing wrong with Walt."

"But he's kind of—kind of different, isn't he?" asked Vince.

"Well, sure, he's got a disability," said Dan, "but that's not wrong."

"I didn't mean that he was bad," said Vince. "I've never seen anyone like him."

"There're lots of people like Walt," said Dan. "He went to a special school where we used to live. It was a big school. Here they just have one small class for people like Walt."

"What do you mean, *like* him?" asked Vince.

"It has different names," said Dan. "But it means that Walt is mentally retarded. He can't learn the same way we do, so he has to learn in different ways."

"Can he learn anything?" asked Vince.

"Sure. Walt can talk so we can understand him," said Dan. "He had to work at it a long time. And he has learned to put on most of his clothes by himself. I've got some games that I can play with him."

"So you don't think anything is wrong with him?" Vince asked again.

"No," said Dan. "He's different, but that's okay. We love Walt and he loves us. We are glad he's in our family."

The two boys continued to look at the caps and try some of them on.

"Will you still be my friend?" asked Dan.

"Why, sure," said Vince. "Why not?"

"I mean if you're my friend, you have to be Walt's friend too," said Dan.

"I guess I've got two new friends," said Vince.

Some Questions

1. Do you know how to talk to, and about, people who are different than you?

2. Can you think of things that you could do to help those who have physical or mental disabilities?

3. Do you think that those who have disabilities could do anything to help you?

Prayer: God, help me to be understanding when I meet someone with a disability. Let that person teach me something too. In Jesus' name. Amen.

 ## Devotion 72

I am writing this to you so that you may know that you have eternal life—you that believe in the Son of God. 1 John 5:13

I Don't Love God

Janelle was talking to her pastor in his office. They talked about school, little sisters, and bugs. Then Pastor Cole asked, "Janelle, do you know why your parents asked the two of us to have this visit?"

"Yes," she answered but said no more.

"Do you want to tell me?" Pastor Cole asked.

"Didn't they tell you?" Janelle asked.

"Yes, but sometimes parents misunderstand things. I thought it would be better for *you* to tell me."

"I don't love God," said Janelle.

"Do you love Jesus?" the pastor asked.

"No," said Janelle, "He's God too."

"I can tell that you pay attention to what you hear in church and Sunday school," said Pastor Cole. "Do you still like to go to Sunday school?"

"Yes," said Janelle, "but I don't love God."

"Did you ever love God?"

"I don't know," said Janelle.

"When did you first decide that you didn't love God anymore?"

"When I found out that Jamie was killed in a car wreck," said Janelle.

This was new information for the pastor. "Who is Jamie?" Pastor Cole asked.

"She was my best friend where we used to live," said Janelle. "Then she died because some drunk driver hit her." Tears formed in Janelle's eyes.

"Are you angry because God let her die?" asked Pastor Cole.

"No," said Janelle. "He didn't let her die. He took her home because she loved Him."

"How do you know that?" the pastor asked.

"My mother said that Jamie loved God, so God took her home to be with Him," explained Janelle.

"Do you think that if you love God, He might take you home too?" asked Pastor Cole.

"Yes," said Janelle.

"So that's why you don't love God anymore?"

"I love my mommy and daddy and my sister and my grandmother and my grandfather and my new friends," said Janelle. "I want to stay with them."

"Jamie didn't die *because* God loved her," said Pastor Cole. "She died because someone did a bad thing and caused a car wreck. God loved her, just as He loves you and your parents and your sister and your grandparents. He doesn't *make* us die because we love Him. But when we do die, He takes us to heaven because Jesus loves us and is our Savior."

"Are you sure?" asked Janelle.

"Real sure," said Pastor Cole. "I've loved Jesus ever since I can remember, and I'm still here."

"Okay," said Janelle as she jumped out of her chair. "Will you explain that to Mommy? I want to be sure she understands too."

Some Questions

1. Do you know that God does not cause people to die?

2. What questions would you like to ask about death or about heaven?

Prayer: Dear Jesus, thank You for loving me and being my Savior. Help me love You and others. Amen.

Devotion 73

I do not claim that I have already succeeded or have already become perfect. I keep striving to win the prize for which Christ Jesus has already won me to Himself.
Philippians 3:12

When I Grow Up

"Grandma, can I ask you something?" Matt asked as he helped his grandmother set the table.

"Sure," said his grandmother.

"When everyone in the family gets here for dinner," said Matt, "I know what they will say to me. They'll ask what I want to be when I grow up."

"I guess adults do ask children that question a lot," said Grandma.

"And I don't know what to say," said Matt. "I don't know what kind of a job I'll have then. I guess I don't even care."

"Well then," said Grandma, "don't talk about jobs. Tell them something else that you want to be when you grow up."

"I don't know what you mean," Matt said.

"You can say, 'When I grow up, I want to be tall like Uncle Harold, funny like Aunt Eva, and kind like my grandfather,' " said Grandma.

"And I want a car like Uncle Ken's," laughed Matt.

"And you want to be a Christian like all of us, I hope," laughed Grandmother.

"And tell stories like my other grandpa," said Matt.

"I think you're ready to answer the questions they'll ask," said Grandma.

"How do you know so much about growing up?" asked Matt. "You did that a long time ago."

"No, I'm still growing up," said Grandma. "I still think about what I want to learn and what I want to do that I haven't done before."

"But you're old," said Matt.

"Sure, I'm old," said Grandmother, "but growing up means learning things, and I can still learn things. So you and I will grow up together. Now get busy. Your Aunt Eva always gets here early, and we want to be ready."

Some Questions

1. What kind of person do you want to be when you grow up?

2. When do you think you will stop growing up?

Prayer: Dear God, help me learn and do things today that will help me all my life. In Jesus' name. Amen.

Devotion 74

It [the tongue] is evil and uncontrollable, full of deadly poison. We use it to give thanks to our Lord and Father and also to curse our fellow-man, who is created in the likeness of God. James 3:8b–9

We Had a Good Drive

Kris and his mother came home after visiting his grandparents. Even though they lived in the same city, it took an hour for them to get home because they had to go through lots of heavy traffic.

"Hi, sweethearts," Kris' father said as they came into the house. "How are your parents?" he asked Kris' mother.

"They're fine," Mom said. "They said to tell you hi and that they were sorry that you couldn't come with us."

"Me too," said Dad, "but I had to get that work done in the garage. Besides, I dread that long drive."

"Actually, we had a good drive today," said Mom. "They've finished the road repair on Grant, so it wasn't as bad as it used to be."

"And there weren't any stupid idiots on the road today," said Kris.

Both of his parents looked at him in surprise.

"What do you mean?" asked his mother.

"When Daddy drives, there are always a lot of stupid idiots driving the other cars," said Kris. "But today there weren't any."

"I think we'd better keep talking about this," said his father.

"And maybe we'd better talk in a different way when we are in heavy traffic," said his mother.

Some Questions

1. What can parents do when they say things that their children should not say?

2. Parents help children. Can children help parents? How?

Prayer: Holy Spirit, let the thoughts that I think
and the words that I say come from You. In
Jesus' name. Amen.

Devotion 75

*Remove my sin, and I will be clean; wash me,
and I will be whiter than snow. Close Your
eyes to my sins and wipe out all my evil.*
Psalm 51:7, 9

I Am Sorry

Tara thought about the things that had happened to her
today. It had started at school. First she was talking to
her friend Anna when the teacher told the class what to
read for social studies. Anna told her to be quiet, but Tara
wanted to tell her friend about something she had heard
at recess. Then the teacher asked Anna to read, and she
didn't know what page the assignment was on. So Anna
was mad at Tara and wouldn't talk to her after school.

When Tara came home from school, she got the milk
out of the refrigerator. When she poured the milk into a
glass, some of it spilled on her older brother's math
assignment. He yelled at her and called her a brat. She
told him he was a jerk.

Tara's mother heard the argument and came into the
kitchen. When she told Tara to clean up the spilled milk,

Tara said she wouldn't do it. Her mother sent her to her room.

Now Tara thought about all the things that had happened. She thought about pretending she was sick so she wouldn't have to see Anna or the teacher the next day. But that would mean she had to stay at home. And Mom was mad at her. Nobody understood her.

Then Mom came into the room.

"Go away," said Tara.

"No, I won't go away," said Mom. "You need someone to love you right now, and I get to do it. Do you know why you are so unhappy now?"

"Because no one likes me," said Tara. "Everyone picks on me."

"Let me say it another way," said Mom. "You did some things that were wrong at school, and you did some things that were wrong at home. We love you, even when you do bad things, but you won't let us help you."

"I don't know what you mean," said Tara.

"We all want to forgive you, but you won't admit you did anything wrong," said Mom. "As long as you think you were right, you can't ask for our help. When you learn to say three important words, you can be happy again."

Tara was quiet for a while. Then she said, "I love you."

"Those are three important words," said Mom. "But even people who love each other can hurt each other. That's why Jesus came to help us. He loves us even when we're wrong, and He forgives us. We ask Him to forgive us when we say three important words. They are, 'I am sorry.' Then we can say the same three words to other people so they can forgive us and we don't have to be unhappy anymore. Those words are like an eraser that wipes everything off a chalkboard."

Tara thought about school the next day. If she said "I am sorry" to Anna, they could be friends again. If she said "I am sorry" to her brother, they could have fun again. She looked at her mother.

"I am sorry," she said.

Some Questions

1. Do you know anyone to whom you need to say, "I am sorry"?
2. Why do you feel better after you say you are sorry?

Prayer: Jesus, my Savior, forgive me my sins as I forgive those who sin against me. Amen.

 ## Devotion 76

But how can they call to Him for help if they have not believed? And how can they believe if they have not heard the message? And how can they hear if the message is not proclaimed? Romans 10:14

Who's Jesus?

When Blair's family moved to a new neighborhood, he was lonesome. Then he found a friend, Nate, who lived across the alley and one house down. Blair asked Nate to come to his house on Saturday afternoon. Blair showed his new friend a secret place he had found in the garage. Someone had put boards across the beams at the top of the garage. It was meant to be a storage place, but it became a great secret hideout for Blair and Nate.

When they finished playing, Nate asked if he could come back the next morning.

"Not in the morning," Blair answered. "I'm going to Sunday school."

"Why do you go to Sunday school?" asked Nate. "Five days of school a week is enough for me."

"But we don't learn about Jesus at regular school," said Blair. "That's why I go to Sunday school."

"Who's Jesus?" asked Nate.

"You don't know who Jesus is?" asked Blair.

"Is he a guy who won a war or something?" asked Nate.

"No," said Blair. "Don't you know about Christmas?"

"We get presents and put up a tree," said Nate.

"But we do it because it's Jesus' birthday," said Blair. "Do you know about Easter?"

"You mean eggs and rabbits?" asked Nate.

"No," said Blair, "I mean about how after Jesus died some people went to His grave and it was empty. He came alive again."

"How do you know all this stuff?" asked Nate.

" 'Cause I go to Sunday school and church," said Blair. "And my mom and dad teach me. I thought everyone knew about Jesus."

"How do you expect me to know about Him if no one ever told me?"

Blair thought about that for a while. Then he said,

"Ask your mother if you can come over tomorrow and go to Sunday school with me. Then we'll go up in our clubhouse and talk about things."

Some Questions

1. How much do you know about Jesus?
2. Do you know anyone who doesn't know Jesus?
3. How could you tell others about the Savior?

> **Prayer:** Holy Spirit, thank You for giving me teachers so I can learn about Jesus. Help me tell my friends about Him too. Amen.

 ## Devotion 77

So I run straight toward the goal in order
to win the prize, which is God's call
through Christ Jesus to the life above.
Philippians 3:14

The Gold Medal for ...

The Clark family enjoyed watching the Olympics together. Each had his or her own favorite event, but they cheered together as they saw the best athletes in the world compete, some winning and some losing.

"Do you think either of you will ever enter the Olympics?" Mr. Clark asked Renee and Noah.

"I'd like to be an ice-skater," said Renee.

"I'm going to be a long-distance runner," said Noah.

"You may both win gold medals," said Mom. "But I think there's something more important than that."

"What is more important than a gold medal at the Olympics?" asked Noah. "You expect me to be president?"

"No," said Mom, "you both have earned gold medals in the family—your Dad has too."

"Hey, I like this," said Dad. "Why do I get a gold medal?"

"To me, you get a gold medal because you spend time with the family," said his wife. "You talk to all of us, and you listen to us. I think that's important."

"How about us?" asked Renee.

"I give you a gold medal because you try hard," said Mom. "I know that you have to work hard at school, but you don't give up. That's worth a gold medal in my book."

"And me?" asked Noah.

"You get a gold medal from me because you have a good sense of humor," said Mom. "You smile a lot, and when you get angry, you don't pout. Instead you tell us why you are angry and go on with it. Gold medal material to me."

"I think we need to tell your mother why we would give her a gold medal," said Dad. "I give you a gold medal, honey, because you are patient with me, and you always encourage me. I need that."

"And I give you a gold medal because you let my friends come over and play even when you are busy and the house is a mess," said Noah.

"I give you a gold medal because you think of fun

things to do," said Renee. "And because you don't make me eat broccoli."

Some Questions

1. What reasons do you have to give gold medals to others in your family? to your friends?

2. For what reasons do you think others might want to give you a gold medal?

Prayer: Dear God, thank You for the good things others do for me. Help me to see the good things I can do for others. In Jesus' name. Amen.

Devotion 78

These are the things you should do: Speak the truth to one another. In the courts give real justice—the kind that brings peace.
Zechariah 8:16

Something to Brag About

Collin was excited when he came home from his Saturday afternoon ball game.

"Look, Mom and Dad," he called as he looked around the house for his parents. "I get to go to baseball camp."

Collin's parents sat down to listen to his excited story. The camp had been planned for several months and was already filled with older players from his team. But Andy Clement's family had to move away, so Collin could go in his place.

"You both have to sign this paper," said Collin, "and then please take me over to the coach's house so he will know that I can go."

Collin's parents started to fill out the paper.

"Whoops, there's a problem here," said Dad.

"It doesn't cost too much, really," said Collin. "I'll even pay some of it out of my allowance if you want."

"That's not the problem," said Dad. "This letter says that you must be 10 years old by the date the camp starts. You won't be 10 until September."

"That doesn't make any difference," said Collin. "I'm big for my age, and I am a good second baseman. The coach wants me to go. Please say my birthday is in June and sign it."

"I want you to go to the camp," said Dad. "But I won't lie to make it happen. You can go next year."

"Mom, will you sign it?" Collin asked.

"No," said Mom. "Your father is right. We love you, and we want to encourage you to be a good ballplayer. But we can't lie."

"You don't really want to help me," yelled Collin. "Everyone else lies all the time. You are old fuddy-duddies who don't even know about the real world." He tried not to cry, but he ran off to his room.

Three days later Collin's mother was in the shopping mall. A lady came up to her and asked, "Aren't you Collin's mother?"

"Yes," she said. "My name is Karen."

"I'm LuAnn," said the other lady. "My son, Robert, is on Collin's baseball team. I wanted to call you last night, but I didn't know your last name."

"What do you need?" asked Karen.

"I just wanted to tell you about a conversation that went on in the back of my van when I drove the team to the game the other night. The boys were talking about going to baseball camp. Collin said he couldn't go because you wouldn't lie for him. The others started to put you down, and I was so proud of the way Collin stood up for you. He bragged that his parents wouldn't lie. He made you sound like such wonderful people that I wanted to meet you."

Some Questions

1. Do you hurt or help another person if you lie for them? Why?

2. What can you do to help someone who wants you to lie for him or her?

Prayer: Dear Jesus, help me tell the truth, even when the truth hurts. Amen.

Devotion 79

Do not let anyone deceive you with foolish words; it is because of these very things that God's anger will come upon those who do not obey Him. Ephesians 5:6

Did He Touch You?

Robyn watched for a time to talk to her mother. She waited until after dinner and until after the kitchen was cleaned up. Then she saw her mother sit down with the newspaper.

"We had a visitor at school today," she told her mother.

"Who was it?" Mom asked.

"A lady from some office like Child's Protective something or other," said Robyn.

"What did she talk about?" asked Mom as she put the newspaper aside.

"She showed us a video about people who try to hurt kids," Robyn explained. "She gave each of us a card with this number—see. She said we should call that number if anyone touched our bodies in places we shouldn't be touched."

"I'm glad she spoke to your class," said Mom. "And I'm glad you told me about it."

"The lady said we should talk to our parents if we were worried about anything," Robyn said.

"And we are talking," said Mom. "Are you worried about anything?"

"I don't think so," said Robyn.

"Has anyone touched your body or said bad things to you?" asked Mom.

"No," said Robyn. "But can I ask you something?"

"Yes," said Mom.

"You know when Uncle Larry comes to visit us," said Robyn, "he always wants me to sit on his lap."

"I hadn't noticed, but I'm glad you told me," said her mother. "Has he touched you in a way that made you feel uncomfortable?"

"No, but I don't like the way he holds me," said Robyn. "I'm too big for that."

"Do you want me to tell him not to do that?" asked Mom.

"No," said Robyn, "but you could ask me to help you do something when he is here. You could help me stay away from him."

"I will do that," said Mom. "And I will keep a close eye on your Uncle Larry. Is there anything else we should talk about?"

"No, that's all," said Robyn.

"Then let's pray about it," Mom answered.

Some Questions

1. Do you know what parts of your body are private and should not be touched by other adults or children?

2. Whom can you talk to if you feel that someone is doing something wrong to you?

Prayer: Dear Father who created my body, thank You for giving me a healthy body. Help me keep my body good and clean, not only with baths but also in how I think about myself. In Jesus' name. Amen.

Devotion 80

The news about Him [Jesus] spread through
the whole country of Syria, so that people
brought to Him all those who were sick, suf-
fering from all kinds of diseases and disor-
ders: people with demons, and epileptics, and
paralytics—and Jesus healed them all.
Matthew 4:24

But He's Disabled

Roni was planning her birthday party. Her parents had told her she could ask seven friends to go with them for a picnic and games in the park. Roni liked to go to the park with her family because there were lots of things to see and do. She wanted to invite all of her friends, so it was difficult for her to pick only seven.

"I've got to invite Sara and Glen 'cause I went to their birthday parties," she said. "And I want Alice and Sissy at my party. Oh, yes, I want to invite Ryan."

"But he has a disability," said her mother.

"What do you mean?" Roni asked.

"His legs are paralyzed, and he has to be in a wheel-chair," said Mom.

"But he goes to school," said Roni. "He plays basket-ball and goes to the mall. I guess he can go to a birthday party."

"Your dad and I have said we will take all of your guests to the park," said her mother. "It would be diffi-cult to take Ryan."

"I don't see why," said Roni. "He can fold up his wheelchair and put it in the car all by himself. I saw him do it."

"But we may want to go on a hike or play some games that require running," said Mom. "I wouldn't want Ryan to feel left out."

"That doesn't bother Ryan a bit," said Roni. "He goes to my Sunday school class too. We had a lesson on how Jesus healed people who couldn't walk. I asked the teacher why Jesus didn't heal Ryan. You know what Ryan said? He said he prayed to be healed, but Jesus gave him a wheelchair and strong arms so he can do almost everything that the rest of us do. Then he said that God gave him interesting things to think about when he can't do what others do."

"Okay, you win," said her mother. "We'll invite Ryan. I'd like to get to know him better."

"Only he might think you have a disability," said Roni.

"Why?"

" 'Cause you're old," teased Roni.

Some Questions

1. How many people do you know who have physical disabilities?

2. How can you help them? How can they help you?

Prayer: Thank You, God, for giving each of us special blessings. Help us use the good things we have to help us live with the problems we have. In Jesus' name. Amen.

Devotion 81

The LORD is in His holy Temple; let every-one on earth be silent in His presence.
Habakkuk 2:20

Why Do We Have to Be Quiet?

Mary enjoyed her Sunday school class. She hugged each of the students as they came into the room. She listened to their stories about pets, brothers and sisters, and school. She had some songs on a tape recorder for the kids to listen to before the class started.

"Okay," Mary said. "It's time for class to start. What's the first thing we do?"

"We pray," said Sharon. John and Nate were still talking about dinosaurs. Three other kids were playing with toys that had been left in a box. Some of the others were talking about what they had seen on TV.

"It's time to pray," said Mary. "So we all have to be quiet."

"Why do we have to be quiet?" asked Jeremy.

"Because we want to pray to God," Mary said.

"But you told us that God can hear us even when we think things in our hearts and that He is always with us to hear our prayers," said Jeremy.

"That's right," said Mary.

"Then why do we have to be quiet?" said Jeremy. "A little noise won't keep God from hearing us."

"Okay, you've got a point," said Mary. "Let's see what the others have to say about this." She asked all of the students to sit down and listen. When they were quiet, Jeremy asked his question again.

"What do you think?" Mary asked. "Do we have to be quiet for God to hear our prayers?"

"No, I think He could hear us even if a hundred million drums were playing and the whole building fell in," said Kristen.

"God could hear us," said Mary. "But could we hear each other?"

"What do you mean?"

"When Jeremy first asked his question, I was the only one who heard it because there was so much noise," said Mary. "You had to be still so we could all hear the question."

"What does that have to do with praying?" asked one of the students.

"God could hear you pray no matter how much noise there was," Mary said. "But you'd have to pray by yourself. If we want to pray together, we have to listen to each other. Okay?"

The students agreed and folded their hands as they closed their mouths.

"Let us pray," said Mary.

Some Questions

1. When do you pray by yourself?
2. When do you pray with others?

Prayer: Thank You, Jesus, for listening to me even when there's lots of noise. Help me to be quiet when I pray with others. Amen.

Devotion 82

Everyone must obey state authorities, because
no authority exists without God's permission,
and the existing authorities have been put
there by God. Romans 13:1

You'll Have Another Chance

Ricky walked into his home after school, still wearing
his bicycle helmet. This was the first week that his parents had allowed him to ride his bike to school. Before
his mom and dad would let him take the bike, he had to
promise that he would come home directly after
school—and that he would always wear his helmet. He
looked at the clock on the microwave. He was home five
minutes early.

"Hi, Ricky," greeted his father. "I've been waiting for
you."

"But look," Ricky protested, "I'm home early."

"That's not the problem," said Dad. "I got off work a
little early too. As I was driving home, I came past the
school, and I saw you riding your bike without your helmet."

"Were you checking on me?" asked Ricky.

"I didn't mean to," said Dad, "but if I would have gone
out of my way to check on you, it would still be the
same. You broke a promise."

"But the other guys don't wear helmets," said Ricky. "I
don't want to look like a sissy."

"In the first place, it is a law that you wear a helmet

when you ride a bike," said Dad. "Even if it were not a local law, your mother and I would make it a family law. We explained that to you."

"But the police didn't stop us," said Ricky.

"I'm not worried about the police," said Dad. "I'm thinking about ambulances. You must obey safety laws for your own protection."

"But the other guys might laugh at me," said Ricky.

"Or they might learn to wear their helmets too," said Dad. "Your mother and I will talk about this tonight. But I am sure that you can't ride your bike to school for at least a week, or maybe two."

"I'm sorry I broke my promise," said Ricky.

"And I forgive you," said Dad. "You'll get another chance. You have to learn to make your own decisions rather than follow the crowd."

"If I wore the helmet while I did homework tonight, would that count?" Ricky asked.

"Good try," said Dad. "But it won't work. Helmets are for bikes. Brains are for homework."

Some Questions

1. How do you feel if someone breaks a promise made to you?

2. Why do governments and families make safety laws?

3. What are the safety rules in your family?

Prayer: Dear God, protect all of us from accidents and dangers. Help us to be careful and not hurt ourselves or others. In Jesus' name. Amen.

Devotion 83

LORD, You have given us Your laws and told us to obey them faithfully. How I hope that I shall be faithful in keeping Your instructions!
Psalm 119:4–5

Who's in Charge?

Darrel was excited because the mailman had brought a box addressed to him. It was a gift from his Uncle Tim and Aunt Julie. He opened it as fast as he could. It was a Transformer! He was eager to play with it, but he discovered that it was not all assembled. As he looked at the parts and the long instructions, he decided to wait until his dad came home to help him.

After dinner he and his father put the box on the table.

"Let's hurry and get it put together," said Darrel. "I want to show it to Chip."

"First, we have to decide who's in charge," Dad said.

"What do you mean?" asked Darrel.

"Am I helping you, or are you helping me?" Dad said. "On my job I've learned that it's important for me to know if I am in charge and need to tell others how to help me or if someone else is in charge to tell me what to do."

"Okay," said Darrel. "I'll be in charge. You help me."

Darrel opened the box and dumped all of the pieces on the table. He picked up a piece and tried to find a place to put it on the Transformer. "You help me," he said to his father.

"What do you want me to do?" Dad asked.

"Put this piece on," Darrel told him.

"Where does it go?" Dad asked.

"I don't know."

"Maybe we need to read the instructions first."

Darrel picked up the instructions and tried to read what they said. He struggled for a while and then said, "I can read, but I can't read this."

"Do you want me to read it for you?" Dad asked.

"Yes," the boy said. "You be in charge, and I'll help you 'cause I can't read all those words."

"You can still be in charge," said Dad. "At my job, if there is something that I can't do, I find someone to help me who can do it. You be in charge, and I'll read the instructions for you."

"Okay," said Darrel, "but read it slowly."

The father and son followed the instructions that came with the toy. Dad read the part that said "IMPORTANT: Put all decals in their proper places before assembling the toy." They put the decals on. Then they followed the rest of the instructions in order.

"Look what I did," Darrel said to his mother. "Dad helped me, but I was in charge. Can I go over and show my Transformer to Chip?"

Some Questions

1. When are you in charge of something and have others help you?

2. When is someone else in charge and you help them?

Prayer: Lord God, help me know when I should follow others and when I should lead others. In Jesus' name. Amen.

Devotion 84

So then, if we have food and clothes, that
should be enough for us. But those who want
to get rich fall into temptation and are caught
in the trap of many foolish and harmful
desires, which pull them down to ruin and
destruction. 1 Timothy 6:8–9

She Has Lots of Money

The day-care director sat on the floor of her office with
Nicole. Ms. Shank was amazed to discover that Nicole
was a pleasant, bright, and loving child. She had just
read reports from several day-care workers that Nicole
caused fights on the playground, called students and
adults bad names, and disrupted quiet times. The director
had called two other day-care centers that Nicole had
attended. She had been expelled from both.

"Do you like being here, Nicole?" she asked.

"Yes, Ms. Shank," said Nicole. "This is the best day
care I've gone to."

"Are you glad to come here in the morning?" asked
Ms. Shank.

"No," the girl answered.

"Why not?"

"Because I'd rather stay home with my mommy," she
said.

"But your mother has to go to work," said the director.

"No, she doesn't," said Nicole. "She said that if I got
kicked out of another day care she'd have to quit her
job."

"Your mother told me that," said Ms. Shank. "But she is a single parent and gets no child support. She has to work to pay the rent and buy food."

"No, she doesn't," answered Nicole.

"Why not?"

"I've got a whole jar full of money," said Nicole. "She can have that to pay the rent and buy groceries."

"Where did you get the money?" asked Ms. Shank.

"When Mommy gives me money to buy something, I don't spend it," said Nicole. I put it in a jar, and it's a big jar. It's almost full. She can use that money, and then we can stay home together."

The director felt tears in her own eyes. Now she understood why Nicole had misbehaved at the other centers.

"Let me show you something," Ms. Shank said to Nicole. She took the child to her desk and opened a cash box.

"See all this money?" she asked Nicole. "That is the money that parents pay me for taking care of their children."

"That's a lot of money," said Nicole.

"Yes, your jar may have $5 or $10 in it," said Ms. Shank. "I have about $200. But even that wouldn't be enough to pay your rent and buy groceries for one month."

Nicole looked at all the money. "I could never save that much, could I?" she asked.

"No, Nicole, you couldn't," said Ms. Shank. "I know you want to help your mother. But your best way of helping her would be to stay in day care so she can keep her job."

"May I stay here?" Nicole asked.

"Yes, we want you here," said Ms. Shank. "Now you go decide which center you'd like to do first."

Some Questions

1. Do you worry about your family having enough money?

2. How can you help your family use their money wisely?

Prayer: Thank You, God, for the money we have. Help us use it in the right way. In Jesus' name. Amen.

 ## Devotion 85

His [Jesus'] parents were astonished when they saw Him, and His mother said to Him, "Son, why have You done this to us? Your father and I have been terribly worried trying to find You." Luke 2:48

I Didn't Do It to You

Dennis was an hour late coming home from school. His parents were scared. They had prayed. They had phoned the school and the police. But no one knew where Dennis was. His father drove around the neighborhood while his mother stayed at home to wait for him. They called all of his friends' parents to see if their children were home. All of them were.

Finally, they saw Dennis walking up the sidewalk

toward their house. They rushed out to hug him and kiss him. They were so relieved to see him and to know that he was okay that for a while they forgot that they were angry with him.

Then they remembered.

"Where have you been?" his mother asked. "We've looked all over for you. We even called the police."

"I just stopped by the mall," said Dennis, "and I got interested in things and forgot about time."

"But we have told you to come home from school immediately," said his father. "You know you are not allowed to go to the shopping center by yourself. We were scared to death. Why did you do this to us?"

"We were worried because we love you," said his mother. "We thought you might have been kidnapped, or hit by a car, or all kinds of things. Why did you do this to us?" she repeated.

"I didn't do it to you," said Dennis.

"What do you mean you didn't do it to us?" asked his father. "We are responsible for you. We had no way of knowing where you were. We were worried sick."

"But I didn't *mean* to do it to you," said Dennis. "I meant to do it for me."

"What did you do for yourself?" his mother asked.

Dennis hung his head.

"I was thinking about me and what I wanted to do. If I would have thought about you, I would have known that you were worried. But I didn't mean to hurt you. I'm sorry I forgot about you and only thought about myself."

Dennis' parents looked at one another with relief. Now that they knew he was safe they could relax. Maybe they could even understand why their son could forget time at the mall.

"Okay," said his mother. "You didn't do it to hurt us. But I know you understand why we were worried. Now let's go have dinner and thank God that you are safe."

Some Questions

1. What happens when you think only about yourself and forget others?

2. How can you help your family so they won't have to worry about you?

   Prayer: Holy Spirit, remember me when I forget others and help me to think about others—and help them to think about me. In Jesus' name. Amen.

 ## Devotion 86

[Jesus said,] "Do not judge others, so that God will not judge you, for God will judge you in the same way you judge others, and He will apply to you the same rules you apply to others." Matthew 7:1–2

They Yelled at Us

Ashley and Katie rushed into the house to see their mother.

"Are you mad at us?" Katie asked.

"No," said Mom. "Should I be?"

"No," answered Ashley.

"Then why did you ask?" wondered Mom.

"Because Mr. Beeson said he was going to call you," said Ashley. "We didn't do anything to his yard."

"We were walking down the sidewalk and didn't take one step into his yard," added Katie.

"Calm down and tell me what happened," said Mom.

"We were coming home from school and minding our own business," said Katie, "when he started to yell at us. He said we had trampled in his flowers and dropped papers in his yard. We didn't do anything like that. Honest!"

"He said he was going to call the police and then call you," said Ashley. "We ran all the way home 'cause we were scared."

"I think I know what happened," said Mom. "I talked to Mrs. Beeson last week. She said that they had been having trouble since school started because some of the students were messing up their yard."

"But we didn't do it!" said Ashley. "Sarah told me that Mrs. Beeson yelled at her for no reason at all yesterday."

"One or two kids did walk in their yard and leave a mess," said Mom. "Now they are blaming all of you children, and that isn't fair."

"Old people sure are grouchy and mean," said Katie.

"Wait a minute," said Mom. "Do you realize that you are making the same mistake the Beesons made?"

"What do you mean?" asked Katie.

"A few children made a mess in their yard, and they are blaming all children," said Mom. "Two older people have yelled at you, and you are blaming all old people."

"They are grouchy," said Ashley, "and they are old."

"Some kids threw litter in their yard," said Mom. "Are all children guilty?"

"No," said Ashley.

"Do you know what it is called when you blame many people for something that only a few did?" asked Mom.

"Dumb?" suggested Katie.

"Maybe," said her mother. "But big people call it prejudice. That means we judge people without knowing them. It is prejudice to say all children are litterbugs. It is prejudice to say all old people are grouchy."

"I thought school was over for the day," said Ashley.

"It is," said her mother. "But one more lesson never hurt anyone."

Some Questions

1. Do you think anyone has blamed you for something that someone else did?

2. Have you blamed groups of people for what only one person did?

   Prayer: Dear Jesus, please be our judge so I do not have to judge others and others do not have to judge me. Amen.

 ## Devotion 87

God will put His angels in charge of you to protect you wherever you go. They will hold you up with their hands to keep you from hurting your feet on the stones. Psalm 91:11–12

Don't You Have a Guardian Angel?

"Hey boys! Watch out!" a voice called in the mall parking lot.

Bobby and Bret, who were busy talking about a new video game they had seen, looked up. A van was backing out of a parking space toward them. Obviously the driver did not see them. They jumped away from the van just in time.

"Wow!" said Bobby. "That was close!"

"Who yelled at us?" asked Bret as he looked around. Many people were there, but no one seemed to be paying any attention to them.

"It must have been Zack," said Bobby.

"Who's Zack?" asked Bret.

"My guardian angel," said Bobby. "Don't you have a guardian angel?"

"Never heard of it. I think someone over there warned us," he said as he pointed to some shoppers.

"Probably so," said Bobby, "but one of them could be Zack."

"You're too old to have pretend friends anymore," said Bret.

"Guardian angels aren't pretend," said Bobby. "They're real. God sends His angels to protect us. Don't you believe in God?"

"Sure I believe in God," said Bret. "But God helps us. He doesn't need angels to do His job."

"Well, I guess He doesn't need us either," said Bobby, "but He made us. And He made angels too."

"How do you know your angel's name is Zack?" asked Bret.

"I guess I made that part up," said Bobby. "But I figure it's easier to ask God for help if I know my angel's name."

"Do you talk to Zack?" asked Bret.

"Of course not!" said Bobby. "I talk to God. He's the one who sends angels to help us."

"Do you think He's got enough angels for everyone?" asked Bret.

"Sure," said Bobby. "He probably needs two angels to watch over you."

Some Questions

1. Do you ask God to protect you and others, even before you know about a danger?

2. Is it okay to be careless because God will send angels to protect you anyway?

Prayer: Almighty God, send Your holy angels to protect me and_____today. In Jesus' name. Amen.

 ## Devotion 88

*Do yourself a favor and learn all you can;
then remember what you learn and you will
prosper. Proverbs 19:8*

I Wish I Had a Job

Tracey's parents were away for the weekend so Mrs. Erickson was staying with her. Tracey liked to talk to Mrs. Erickson.

"I wish I had a job," Tracey said.

"What kind of job would you like?" asked Mrs. Erickson.

"I don't know," said Tracey. "That's why I want a job. I'm bored."

"Oh, you must never be bored," said Mrs. Erickson. "Life is too important to waste even a moment being bored."

"But I don't have anything interesting to do," Tracey said.

"But you do have something to do," said the older woman. "Right now you have one of the most important jobs in your life."

"But I don't have a job," Tracey protested.

"Think of the things you are supposed to do," said Mrs. Erickson. "That is your job."

"You mean going to school, don't you?" asked Tracey. "That's supposed to be my job."

"Going to school is part of your job," Mrs. Erickson said, "but not all of it."

"But what good is it to learn all that history and math and junk?" Tracey asked. "I'm not going to do that kind of stuff when I grow up."

"But you don't learn things just to get a job to make money," said Mrs. Erickson. "You learn things so you can understand people. When you know things, you won't be bored because you have interesting things to think about."

"But school is boring too," said Tracey.

"You will not be bored if you are not boring," said Mrs. Erickson. "School is teaching you more than history, math, and the other things you call junk. You need to learn how to get along with people, how to think and make decisions, how to be honest and fair. Those things are all your job now. It's an important job."

"But who is teaching me those kinds of things?" asked Tracey.

"Everyone is," said Mrs. Erickson. "The teacher in your classroom is only one of the many people who teach you. Your job is to watch people. Some people teach you by showing you good things. Others teach you by doing things that aren't good, and you learn from them not to make the same mistakes. You can learn a lot of things by listening to people."

"How did you learn so much?" asked Tracey.

"I have always spent a lot of time with kids," said Mrs. Erickson. "They have been some of my best teachers."

Some Questions

1. What can you do when you feel bored?

2. You have teachers in school and Sunday school. Who else teaches you about life?

Prayer: Thank You, God, for all the interesting people in my life. Help me to learn from them, and help me teach them. In Jesus' name. Amen.

Devotion 89

I have learned this secret, so that anywhere,
at any time, I am content, whether I am full
or hungry, whether I have too much or too lit-
tle. I have the strength to face all conditions
by the power that Christ gives me.
Philippians 4:12b–13

I Didn't Make It

Raymond watched as the principal's secretary came into his classroom and gave his teacher a note. Today was the day he had been looking forward to for three weeks. It had been that long since half of the kids in his class took a special test. Those who scored high on the test would be invited to go to a special school next year. His dad had called the other school a "fast track." Raymond knew it was important to his parents for him to get into that school. His mother said it guaranteed that he could go to any college he wanted.

The teacher asked two students, Johanna and Jeff, to go to the principal's office. Raymond knew what that meant. He had not scored high enough on the test.

"Raymond, would you please come up here?" Miss Garland said. The class was supposed to be doing a reading assignment. Raymond assumed that the teacher noticed he hadn't been reading.

"You didn't look as if you were reading, Raymond," she said.

"I didn't pass the special test, did I?" Raymond asked.

"Of course you passed it," said Miss Garland. "I'm sure you did well, but not well enough to go to the special school next year." She saw tears in Raymond's eyes.

"Do I have to tell my parents or will you?" he asked.

"You can tell them," she said. "But if you want, I will phone them."

"I guess you can't make them feel any better either," Raymond said. The tears now rolled down his cheeks.

"I will tell your mother and father that there is another test more important than the one you took three weeks ago," said Miss Garland.

"What test is that?" Raymond asked.

"It is the test you give yourself," said the teacher. "I'm proud of Johanna and Jeff for getting into the special school, but I'm just as proud of you. You work hard. You are kind to people. The other kids like to have you in the class. I hope you know those things about yourself."

"I feel like I'm a failure today," said Raymond.

"You are not a failure," said Miss Garland. "Lots of the students in the class didn't even take the test you did. They aren't disappointed because they didn't even try. You tried and you did well. You learned a lot about yourself. You've given me a chance to tell you that you are a fine person."

"Thank you, Miss Garland," Raymond said.

"You're welcome," she said. "I'll call your parents tonight after you've had a chance to talk to them."

Some Questions

1. Are you afraid to try something new because you think you can't do it?

2. Can you win without bragging?

3. Can you lose without feeling that you are no good?

Prayer: Holy Spirit, help me understand myself so I may try hard to do many things and learn something when I find I can't do everything. In Jesus' name. Amen.

 ## Devotion 90

*Our brothers, we want you to know the truth
about those who have died, so that you will
not be sad, as are those who have no hope.
We believe that Jesus died and rose again,
and so we believe that God will take back
with Jesus those who have died believing in
Him. 1 Thessalonians 4:13–14*

Why Did You Go to a Funeral?

"Hey, Jerry," Sean called. "Why weren't you in school yesterday afternoon? I saw you in the morning."

"I went to my grandmother's funeral," Jerry said.

"My dad says that where he works people who want to goof off say they are going to their grandmother's funeral," said Bill.

"I really went to her funeral," said Jerry.

"Why?" asked Bill.

"Because she died, stupid," said Jerry. "Why do you think?"

"But you didn't have to go," said Bill. "Funerals are spooky things."

"I've never been to one," said Sean, "but I've heard they are sad."

"Sure it was sad," said Jerry. "I'm going to miss my grandmother a lot. But it helps to go to a funeral."

"I've never been to one," said Sean, "and I don't plan to go either."

"Me either," said Bill. "What do they do at funerals?"

"I've been to two funerals," said Jerry. "Our neighbor died two months ago. Mom wanted me to go. I think she had figured out that Grandma was going to die soon, and she wanted me to know about funerals."

"Well, what do they do?" asked Sean.

"It was in church," said Jerry. "We didn't get to sit where we usually do. Because we were family, we had to sit up front. They sang some songs, such as 'Jesus Lives! The Victory's Won' and 'He's Risen,' and things like that."

"That doesn't sound so sad," said Bill. "Did you see your grandmother in the casket?"

"I did in the funeral home, but the casket was closed in the church," said Jerry. "They had some flowers on it. Then the pastor talked about dying. He said that he was glad my cousins and I knew how Jesus had died for us and rose again. He said Grandma believed in Jesus and was with Him in heaven."

"Do you believe that?" Bill asked.

"Sure, don't you?" asked Jerry.

"I don't know," said Bill. "I've never thought about it."

"What else happened?" asked Sean.

"We went out to the cemetery where they buried her later," said Jerry. "Then we all went over to Aunt Clara's house and ate supper. At first I had to talk to all the relatives, but then I got to play with my cousins."

"My family doesn't go to church," said Bill. "What would we do if my grandmother died?"

"I don't know," said Jerry. "But you can come to church with my family if you want. We won't sit in the front row."

Some Questions

1. What do you know about funerals?

2. Do you want to ask any questions about funerals or burial?

Prayer: Dear Jesus, thank You for living for us, dying for us, and living again. When we are sad about dying, help us have hope because You are our Savior. Amen.

 Devotion 91

Finally, our brothers, you learned from us how you should live in order to please God. This is, of course, the way you have been living. And now we beg and urge you in the name of the Lord Jesus to do even more.
1 Thessalonians 4:1

It's Your Choice

"Mom! Mom! Guess what!" Kelsey called as she ran into the house. "Laura's parents have invited me to go with them on a trip this weekend. Can I go? Can I go?"

"That's nice that they invited you," said Kelsey's mother.

"Mrs. Clark said for you to call her, and she'd give you all the details," Kelsey said. She knew that all parents wanted to know the details.

"But haven't you forgotten one of the details already?" asked Kelsey's mother.

"What?" Kelsey asked.

"You promised Mrs. Jackson that you would take care of her cat and houseplants this weekend," said her mother. "In fact, she has already paid you for doing the job."

"I'll give the money back to her," said Kelsey.

"It's not that easy," said Mom. "The cat and the house-plants need care. Mrs. Clark is depending on you."

"You're not going to let me go, are you?" asked Kelsey.

"I guess I could just tell you that you can't go because you have promised Mrs. Jackson to help her," said Mom. "But maybe it's time you learn to take responsibility for yourself. It's your choice."

"You mean that I get to decide which one I will do?" asked Kelsey.

"Yes," said her mother, "but I want to help you think about some things before you decide."

"Like what?" Kelsey asked.

"Mrs. Jackson paid you to do something," Mom said.

"That's like a job, a real job. That means Mrs. Jackson thinks you are a responsible person. Your father and I have jobs. We can't just tell our bosses that we aren't coming to work."

"But you are adults," protested Kelsey.

"That doesn't always make a difference," said Mom. "Some adults don't accept responsibility, maybe because they didn't learn when they were kids. I want you to learn to be a responsible person."

"Maybe I could get someone else to take care of Mrs. Jackson's cat and plants," said Kelsey.

"Maybe," said her mother. "But you would have to find someone who is very responsible. If that person did not do a good job, it would be your fault."

"Why don't you tell me what to do?" asked Kelsey.

"No, Mrs. Jackson thought you were responsible," said Mom. "Some day when you are an adult, you will need someone to give you a reference. Do you know what that is?"

"That's when someone writes a letter and says you would be good for a job or for school," said Kelsey.

"Right," said Mom. "Some day you may want Mrs. Jackson to write a letter to recommend you for something much more important than a weekend with your friend."

"But I really want to go with Laura's family," said Kelsey.

"I understand," said her mother. "It's your choice."

Some Questions

1. What do you think Kelsey decided to do?

2. Think of times when you had to make a choice. Did you make good decisions?

Prayer: Holy Spirit, help me know the way to live so I know how to make up my mind the right way. In Jesus' name. Amen.

 ## Devotion 92

And so, in honor of the name of Jesus all beings in heaven, on earth, and in the world below will fall on their knees, and all will openly proclaim that Jesus Christ is Lord, to the glory of God the Father.
Philippians 2:10–11

What Did You Say?

Mrs. Crawford stood at her kitchen sink in the small mobile home where her family of four lived. She watched her son, Robert, playing outside the window. She was sad.

Her family had lived in the mobile home for three months—since her husband had lost his job. There had been several shootings in the park. She knew that even some children had guns. She knew that her children were hearing and seeing things that would hurt them. She felt she could not protect her own children from what was happening.

"Lord," she prayed, "help my husband find a job today."

Mrs. Crawford watched Robert as he climbed up on a garbage can. He was almost 3 years old and had not spoken a word yet. She knew she should get help for him, but she couldn't afford to go to a doctor. She knew he could hear. He liked to listen to music. He did the things that others asked him to do. But he never talked.

She had one hope. For the last six weeks Robert had been going to Sunday school in the garage in the center of the mobile home park. Some people from a church in the next town taught the classes. Robert liked to go to Sunday school. After three weeks the Sunday school teacher had come to her home. At first Mrs. Crawford was ashamed of how poor her home was. But she forgot her embarrassment when she realized that the teacher cared about Robert. The teacher said he never sang a song. He never caused any problems. He just sat there. The teacher was afraid that he wasn't learning anything.

From the window Mrs. Crawford heard other children playing. They were using filthy and profane words. How long would they have to live here? Then she heard Robert say something. Very clearly he said, "Jesus." His first word had to be a curse! She was angry at herself, and at her husband, because they lived where her little boy was exposed to such language. She grabbed a bar of soap from the sink and ran outside. She would wash his mouth out with soap. That would teach him not to speak that way.

"What did you say?" she said to Robert as she held the soap in front of his face.

Then he spoke his first sentence.

"I said, 'Jesus loves me,' " Robert said.

Some Questions

1. Do you hear other people say things that you should not say?

2. How can you talk about Jesus so people will know that you love Him?

   Prayer: Lord Jesus, I am glad You know my name and I know Yours. Amen.

 ## Devotion 93

Don't be fools, then, but try to find out what the Lord wants you to do. Ephesians 5:17

What Does God Want Me to Do?

Glenda had to make a choice. Her friend Susan had invited her to go on a fishing trip with her family. She liked Susan's family, and she knew she would have a good time, even if they didn't catch any fish.

But Glenda's grandparents had invited her to spend the same weekend with them. She knew they would take her shopping and out to lunch. Maybe they would even take her to the theme park where she liked to ride the cars and boats.

Glenda had already asked her mother to help her decide if she should go fishing with Susan's family or if she should spend the weekend with Grandpa and Grandma. But her mother said that this time it was her choice. Her mother suggested that she think about it and pray about it.

First Glenda thought about it. She knew that Susan's family couldn't change the weekend because they had rented a boat. She asked her grandmother if they could change the weekend, but she found out that her grandfather had to work on most Saturdays. He had this Saturday free and wanted to be with Glenda when she was out of school. Thinking about it didn't seem to help. So she decided to pray.

"Dear God," she prayed, "tell me what to do."

She didn't hear God answer her prayer.

"I prayed to God," she told her mother, "but He didn't tell me what I should do."

"Remember the verse from the Scripture you learned in Sunday school," her mother said. "It said, 'Try to find out what the Lord wants you to do.' "

"I did that," Glenda said. "I asked Him to tell me, but He didn't."

"Maybe God wants you to make up your own mind," said her mother.

"Why?" Glenda asked.

"If God told you to be with your grandparents, Susan would feel that God didn't care about her. On the other hand, if God told you to be with Susan, your grandparents would think God didn't like them."

"But that's how I feel if I have to decide," said Glenda.

"Now you understand why God sent His Son, Jesus, to be a human being like us," said her mother. "God doesn't tell us what to wear and where to go. He gave us brains so we can make decisions. Remember, I told you to think about your problem and pray about it."

"I did," said Glenda, "but I still don't know what to do."

"But you do know what God wants," said her mother. "He wants you to love both your friend and your grandparents. God wants you to help other people and to let other people help you. He wants you to have a good time, and He also wants you to help other people have a good time. Can you think of other things that God wants you to do?"

"Yes," said Glenda. "He wants me to say I'm sorry when I do something wrong. He wants me to forgive others. So that means, even if I don't always do the right thing, He will help me start over and do better the next time."

"I'm glad you know that, Glenda," said her mother. "You know how to think and to pray. God will be with you to help you whatever you decide to do."

Some Questions

1. If you were Glenda, what would you choose to do?

2. How will God help you when you need to make a decision?

Prayer: Dear God, help me know more about You so I may know how to make up my mind about things. In Jesus' name. Amen.

Devotion 94

[Jesus said,] "For only a penny you can buy two sparrows, yet not one sparrow falls to the ground without your Father's consent. ... So do not be afraid; you are worth much more than many sparrows!" Matthew 10:29, 31

I'm Scared

"Hey, Jeannie," her father called one Saturday morning, "I'm going down to the shopping center. Want to go along?"

"No, thank you," Jeannie answered from her room.

Her father walked down the hall and looked into the room to see his daughter playing a video game.

"It won't take me very long to buy the paint that I need," he said. "Then we might have time for a frozen yogurt."

"I'd rather not go today," Jeannie said. She continued to look at the video screen.

"You don't want to ride in the car, do you?" Dad asked.

Jeannie sat looking at the game without playing for a long time. Finally, she said, "I'm scared."

"I understand," Dad said. "Let's talk about it." He reached over and turned off the video game and held his daughter's hand.

Two days before, Jeannie had been riding home from choir practice at church with her friend Connie. A drunk driver ran a red light and hit the car that Jeannie was riding in. Jeannie was wearing a seat belt and was not hurt seriously, but she had to ride in an ambulance to the Urgent Care center. Connie had a broken arm and Connie's mom was still in the hospital.

"I can understand why you don't want to ride in the car, right now," said Dad. "But I also want to help you understand that accidents can happen anywhere, even in our home."

"But when I get in a car, I still think about all those things," Jeannie said, "and I'm scared."

"I would be too," said Dad. "Remember the Bible verse on the Sunday school lesson you brought home a couple of weeks ago? It said that God knows and cares about everything, even the sparrows. He is always with you, so you don't have to be afraid."

"But Connie and her mother believe in Jesus," she said, "and they got hurt."

"Yes, they were hurt," her dad said, "and we thank God they will both get well. Jesus does not promise us that bad things will not happen to us, but He does promise that He will be with us no matter what happens."

"Even if we get killed?" Jeannie asked.

"Yes, even if we get killed," Dad said. "Jesus died and rose again, so He has power over death. Even when we die, He is with us, and He will take us to heaven."

"But I don't want to go yet," Jeannie said.

"And I want to keep you here too," said her dad, "so we'll wear our seat belts and ask God to protect us."

"Can we have ice cream instead of yogurt?" Jeannie asked as she got up and took her father's hand to go down the hall toward the car.

Some Questions

1. Do you have bad dreams or worry sometimes that something bad might happen?

2. Whom can you talk to about the things that scare you?

3. What do you think about when you pray "deliver us from evil" in the Lord's Prayer?

   Prayer: Dear Jesus, be with us and with_____ and protect us from all the bad things that might happen. And help us enjoy the good things that happen. Amen.

Devotion 95

[God asked,] "Did you eat the fruit that I told you not to eat?" The man answered, "The woman You put here with me gave me the fruit, and I ate it." Genesis 3:11b–12

Who's to Blame?

Ryan was happy about the basketball that his Uncle Al gave him for his birthday. It was a real basketball, like the ones they used in games he watched on TV. His dad and Uncle Al had put up a hoop for him on the back side of the garage.

One Saturday Ryan and three of his friends played basketball until they were tired. Ryan's mother brought some lemonade and cookies for them behind the garage. They sat around and talked about stuff until Ryan's friends went home.

After church on Sunday Ryan went to the garage to look for his basketball. It was not there. Then he remembered that he had forgotten to put the ball away after they had finished playing the day before. He went out in the yard to look for the ball. He couldn't find it. He told his parents, and they helped him look. But the ball was gone. Someone must have seen it in the yard and taken it.

"It's my friends' fault," said Ryan. "They played with my basketball at my house. They should have helped me put it away. They have to help me pay for it."

"No," said Ryan's mother. "You played at our house, and you were responsible for the ball."

"Then it's your fault," Ryan said to his parents. "You didn't tell me to put the ball away. And Mom made me forget because she brought out treats for us."

"Wait a minute," said Dad. "You can't blame other people. You need to learn to be responsible for yourself. You left the ball out in the yard. That doesn't make you a bad person. We all make mistakes, but we have to learn from our mistakes. If you blame someone else, you'll never learn. If you admit that you left the ball out, then you can ask God to help you change and be more careful."

"Can I ask Uncle Al to buy me another basketball?" Ryan asked.

"No," said his mother. "He gave you a nice present. But you can use your allowance money, and I'm sure we can find some jobs for you to do so you can earn some extra money. Then you can buy another basketball. And then you'll take good care of it."

Some Questions

1. Do you agree that Ryan was responsible and should buy a new ball by himself? Why or why not?

2. Can you think of times when you tried to blame others for a mistake you made?

Prayer: Dear God, thank You for all the good things that I have. Help me take good care of them and be responsible for what I do. In Jesus' name. Amen.

 ## Devotion 96

O LORD, our LORD, Your greatness is seen in all the world! Your praise reaches up to the heavens; it is sung by children and babies. Psalm 8:1–2

We're Going to Have a Baby!

Colin couldn't wait until his grandparents' wedding anniversary when he knew all of his family would be together. He liked to play with his cousins. Even though he was the youngest one, they always let him play with them.

On the big day the adults stayed in the house but the kids went out to the yard to play. Then Colin made his big announcement.

"We're going to have a baby!" he said.

"Who's going to have a baby?" asked one of the older cousins.

"We are!" he answered.

"You mean Aunt Jane is going to have a baby," the cousins corrected.

"Sure, she is," said Colin, even though it seemed strange to hear his mother called Aunt Jane. "But Daddy and I are going to have a baby too."

"Daddies don't have babies," another cousin said. "Mothers have babies."

"Daddies do have babies," said Colin. "Just 'cause you're older than I am doesn't mean you're so smart. I know mothers can't have babies without fathers."

"Okay," said the first cousin. "Your parents are going to have a baby, but you aren't."

"I am too going to have a baby," said Colin.

"Little boys don't have babies," said another cousin. Colin was happy because he saw that all of his cousins had stopped playing and were listening in on the conversation.

"Yes, I can," said Colin. "I can have a little sister, or maybe a little brother. We don't know which yet. Just like my mommy and daddy will have a son or daughter, I will have a brother or sister, so I will have a baby."

"I think that's dumb," said one of the older cousins.

"I think it's nice," said another.

"I think we had better play ball now," said another. " 'Cause when they say dinner is ready, I'm out of here."

Some Questions

1. Do you know about the day you were born? about the day you were baptized? Ask your parents to tell you about it and show you pictures.

2. If you do not have brothers and sisters, uncles and aunts, or cousins, can you find other friends who seem like family for you?

Prayer: Dear God, thank You for every member of my family. Please, God, also help them be thankful that I am related to them. In Jesus' name. Amen.

 ## Devotion 97

[Jesus said,] "Listen! I am sending you out just like sheep to a pack of wolves. You must be as cautious as snakes and as gentle as doves." Matthew 10:16

I Want to Go to the Library

Ashley rushed into the house. She threw her backpack on the floor and started calling for her mother.

"I'm here," her mother answered. "I know you're hungry. There's juice in the fridge and a banana on the table for you."

"I'm not hungry," said Ashley. "I want to go to the library right now."

Ashley's mother walked into the kitchen. She could see that her daughter was very upset. .

"What's wrong?" she asked.

"I want to go to the library and get a book about karate," Ashley answered.

"Why are you suddenly interested in karate?" asked her mother.

"Some big kids picked on me while I was waiting for the bus," Ashley answered. "They called me dumb names and tried to trip me. I'm going to learn karate, and I'll show them a thing or two."

"Did they hurt you?" her mother asked.

"They didn't hurt my outside," she said, "but they hurt my insides."

"I understand that," Mom said. "Do you know who they were?"

"I don't know their names, but I've seen them before," said Ashley. "They are in middle school. There were three of them, and they were all bigger than me. If I know karate, I can protect myself."

"That would be one way," said her mother. "Do you think there could be other ways?"

"I don't care about other ways," said Ashley.

"I want to help you," said Mom. "The school and the bus driver also want to help you. If you want to learn karate, that's fine. But it will take awhile. We want to help you right now."

Ashley stopped to think. She had not thought about how long it might take to learn to protect herself.

"Tell you what," said Mom, "I'll call the school tomorrow and see what I can do. We'll be going to the library next week anyway. If you want the book on karate then, we'll look for one."

Some Questions

1. Do you feel you need someone to protect you at school

or other places?

2. How can you get help?

3. How can you help others who may also be afraid?

Prayer: Lord, deliver us from evil—the evil of mean people, the evil of gangs, the evil of bullies. In Jesus' name. Amen.

 ## Devotion 98

[Jesus said,] "I am the good shepherd. As the Father knows Me and I know the Father, in the same way I know My sheep and they know Me. And I am willing to die for them."
John 10:14–15

A Time to Be Alone

Christina walked slowly up the steps to the front door. She put the key into the lock and turned it. She remembered how she had begged her parents to let her come home after school rather than stay in the day-care center. She had told them how responsible she would be. She showed them that she knew how to call 911. She promised not to invite any friends to come home with her. Finally, her parents had agreed that she was grown up enough to stay home by herself for the hour before her mother came home.

Now Christina was sorry she had talked her parents into letting her stay home alone. She was not scared to be home by herself. Her parents had told her that they were proud of the way she took care of herself. She liked wearing the key to the house around her neck all day at school.

But today she was lonely. One of her best friends at school had moved away. Christina missed Crystal. Then today she'd made a mistake when she presented her science project to the class. Some of the kids laughed at her. She spilled ketchup on her blouse at lunch. Even though she had tried to wash the spot out in the bathroom, she could still see it and was sure everyone else could too.

Christina walked into the kitchen. She knew there was a snack for her somewhere, but she wasn't hungry. She usually turned on some music, but today she forgot. She wished one of her parents would come home early. Then she worried that they might come home later than usual.

She went into her room and looked on the top shelf of her closet. There she saw the stuffed dog that she used to hold when she felt lonely. For a moment she thought about pulling the dog down and holding it on her bed. But she thought she might fall asleep and her parents would come home and find her with the stuffed dog. She left it where it was.

As Christina walked through the dining room, she saw that her mother had left the big tablecloth on the table but had dropped the side leaves. The tablecloth reached almost to the floor.

Again she remembered what she had done when she was a little girl. This time she did it.

Christina crawled under the table. She remembered how this used to be one of her hiding places when she was little. It was a place where she could feel safe and think about herself. The space under the table seemed smaller now, but she liked that. It was a room made for her—not for adults.

She remembered how she used to pray when she was alone under the table. She tried again. "Dear Jesus," she prayed, "thank You for being with me. Please bless Crystal in her new school. Help me have fun with others even when things don't go right. And help me think about others when they are alone."

Christina didn't say "amen" to her prayer. Instead she rested with her back on a table leg. If she said "amen," it would seem as though her visit with Jesus were over. And it wasn't.

Some Questions

1. Are there times when you need to be alone?
2. When and where do you like to talk to God?

Prayer: Come, Lord Jesus, talk to me. Amen.

 ## Devotion 99

Words of thanksgiving and cursing pour out from the same mouth. My brothers, this should not happen! James 3:10

I Wasn't Talking about the Other Kids

Little League baseball practice was over. The coach was putting away the bats and balls. All the other players had gone, but Joshua stood near home plate.

"Your folks late picking you up, Josh?" the coach asked.

"No," he answered. "I walk home." The coach suspected that Josh was staying late because he wanted to talk about something.

"I know this is your first year on the team," the coach said. "Are you enjoying it?"

"Oh, yes!" Joshua said. He was glad the coach had started a conversation. He had practiced over and over what he wanted to say. Now was his chance.

"There is one thing that kinda bothers me though," Joshua said.

"What's that, son?" the coach said as he squatted near the young boy.

"I'm not a sissy or anything like that," Joshua said, "but I go to Sunday school and believe in God, and I pray and things like that."

"That's fine, Josh," said the coach. "I'm glad you do those things."

"It kind of bothers me," said Joshua, as he said aloud the words he had practiced all day long, "when people use God's name to mean bad things. I mean I can get along with some bad words, but I don't like to hear people use God's name to hurt others."

"I'm glad you can talk to me about that," said the coach. "I understand. But you've got to understand that some of these kids don't have a Christian home as you do. They've heard some pretty bad things, so I guess it's natural that they say those things."

"I wasn't talking about the kids," Joshua said very quietly.

The coach sat quietly for a long time. Finally, he said, "You're talking about me?"

"Yeah," said Joshua. "You and the guy who helps you."

"You're a brave little tiger, Josh," said the coach. "I like you. Tell you what, I'll coach you about baseball, and you coach me about the God stuff you were talking about. Okay?"

"Fine with me," said Joshua. "Now I've got to get home 'cause my mom will wonder where I am."

Some Questions

1. How do you hear God's name used at school? with your friends? at home?

2. How do you use God's name?

Prayer: God, every time I use Your prayer I say, "Hallowed be Your name," but this time I want to especially ask You to help me use Your name in a holy way. In Jesus' name. Amen.

Devotion 100

Even if I go through the deepest darkness, I will not be afraid, LORD, for You are with me. Your shepherd's rod and staff protect me.
Psalm 23:4

Waiting

Sharon stood at the exact place her mother had told her to wait. She knew that she was there at the right time.

Her mother had an appointment with a dentist on a Saturday afternoon and had planned to get a baby-sitter for Sharon. But Sharon had told her mother that it would cost less money for her to go to a movie instead of getting the sitter.

At first her mother said no. Then they talked some more. The movie started about an hour before the dental appointment. Her mother could help her get into the theater, and she would be safe there. Then her mother could do some shopping, go to the dentist, and pick up Sharon after the movie.

Sharon had enjoyed the movie. It was funny, and it was the first time she'd been allowed to go by herself. She was eager to tell her mom about the movie. She kept watching for her mother's car. Time went by. She saw several blue cars that looked just like their car, but each time the car drove right by her.

After a while, Sharon started to feel angry at her mother. Why is she leaving me standing here by myself? she thought. Then she realized that her mother would not do that. Her mother was fussy about being on time.

Then Sharon worried that she had misunderstood her mother. Maybe she was supposed to wait on the other side of the theater. But she remembered her mother showing her the sign that was behind her. She was in the right place.

A man drove by very slowly in a car. He saw Sharon and turned around and drove by again. This time he stopped and offered to give her a ride. She remembered what she had learned in school about strangers. She said no very loudly and walked back toward the theater. The car drove away.

She saw four teenage guys looking at her from the other side of the sidewalk. She was afraid. Then she saw a security guard and walked toward him. The boys saw the guard and left.

Then Sharon started worrying about her mother. Maybe she had been in a wreck. Hadn't she heard an ambulance when she first came out of the theater? What if her mother were in the hospital? What if she were killed? She prayed and asked God to protect her mother. Tears started streaming down Sharon's face.

Should she ask a stranger for help? Her mother always told her to have a quarter to make a phone call. She knew where a phone was, but she didn't know who to call.

Then she heard a horn honk. There was her mother driving toward her!

She rushed to the car and jumped in. Her mother had tears in her eyes too. They hugged each other.

"Oh, darling," her mother said, "I was so worried about you. When I came out of the dentist's office, I had a flat tire. I couldn't get anyone to help me, so I had to change it myself. I rushed as fast as I could. I kept praying for you. I hope you weren't worried."

Some Questions

1. If you were Sharon, what would you have done as you waited?

2. Have you worried because you had to wait for someone?

3. Have others in your family worried as they waited for you?

Prayer: Dear God, please protect us from all the things that scare us. In Jesus' name. Amen.

 ## Devotion 101

For it is by God's grace that you have been saved through faith. It is not the result of your own efforts, but God's gift, so that no one can boast about it. God has made us what we are, and in our union with Christ Jesus He has created us for a life of good deeds, which He has already prepared for us to do.
Ephesians 2:8–10

Who's the Duty Kid?

Jonathan, Jared, and Heidi were finally all in bed. Because it was a school night their parents knew that all three would soon be asleep and the house would be quiet. The parents sat down together before their favorite TV program came on.

"Did you see what Jared did tonight?" their father asked his wife.

"I saw so many things they did that I can't remember them all," their mother answered. "And I'm sure I missed a few things at that."

"I was already home from work and sitting in the den when I heard the evening paper land on the porch," Dad said. "I was trying to talk myself into finding the energy to go out for the paper when Jared brought it in for me.

And it's not even report card week."

"And allowances aren't due until Friday," their mother said.

"Jonathan did the same thing last week, and I forgot to tell you," said Dad. "And Heidi pulled my shoes off and brought me a glass of tea while I was reading the paper. They're great kids."

"Of course, they are," said their mother. "I know you're tired when you get home. If you want the kids to bring the paper in for you every day so you can rest, you should ask them to do it for you."

"I thought about that," said Dad. "I thought I'd name a duty kid to bring in the paper for each day, but I decided not to."

"Why not?"

"Because if I made them do it, they'd lose the fun of doing it because they want to," said Dad. "I'd rather they get it for me when they want to, not because they have to."

Some Questions

1. What do your parents do for you because they want to? Do they do some things because they have to?

2. What do you do for your family because you want to? What do you do because you have to?

Prayer: Thank You, God, for letting me help You and the people in my family and at school. Help me love people so I can help them because I want to make them happy. In Jesus' name. Amen.

DATE DUE			